# Curators' Focus:
## *Turning In Context*

[Physical, Emotional, Spiritual and Intellectual]

Albert LeCoff
*Executive Director*

Wood Turning Center
*Philadelphia*

**Curators' Focus:** *Turning In Context*

The Wood Turning Center of Philadelphia is a nonprofit membership organization founded in 1976 dedicated to the education, preservation, and promotion of the art and craft of lathe turning through organizing exhibitions, conferences, symposia, and outreach programs. The center's goal is to encourage and promote the work of established and developing artists and to cultivate among the public a deeper understanding and appreciation of lathe turning.

Contact the Wood Turning Center for more information about this book and exhibition, other publications produced by the center, or the art of lathe turning.

P.O. Box 25706
Philadelphia, PA 19144 USA
Telephone 215-844-2188
Fax 215-844-6116
E-mail woodturning@compuserve.com
http://www.libertynet.org:80/~woodturn

©1997 by the Wood Turning Center, Inc.
P.O. Box 25706, Philadelphia, PA 19144 USA
All rights reserved

Library of Congress Cataloging-in-Publication Data:

Curators' focus: turning in context: physical, emotional, spiritual, and intellectual/Albert LeCoff, executive director.
    p. cm.
    Exhibition catalog.
    Includes bibliographical references.
    ISBN 0-9624385-8-8 (pbk.)
    1. Woodwork—History—20th century—Themes, motives—Exhibitions. 2. Turning—Technique—Exhibitions. I. LeCoff, Albert B., 1950-.
NK9710.C87   1997
745.51'07473—dc21                              97-34004
                                                        CIP

# Contents

**Acknowledgements**   5

**Introduction**   6

**Preface**
Turning to the Culture of Memory
*Stephen Hogbin*   7

**Physical Context**
Notes on the Physical
*Bruce Metcalf*   18

**Emotional Context**
Fascination for the Circle:
Form, Expression, and Beauty
*Maria van Kesteren*   26

**Spiritual Context**
Myths, Icons, and Beliefs
*Mark Richard Leach*   34

**Intellectual Context**
Eye, Hand, and Mind
Turning as Art, as Craft, as History, as Thought
*David Revere McFadden*   42

**How and Why**
*William P. Daley*   52

**Turning, Now and Then**
*Albert LeCoff*   58

**Exhibition Catalogue**   60

*Lisa Tremper Barnes,* Director
**Philip and Muriel Berman Museum of Art,
at Ursinus College**

The collaboration between the Wood Turning Center and the Philip and Muriel Berman Museum of Art had its genesis in our presentation of the exhibition *Challenge V: International Lathe-Turned Objects* in January 1994. Since that time, the two organizations have developed an ongoing relationship committed to the exhibition, documentation and scholarship of the art of lathe turning. Each August the Berman Museum presents an exhibition devoted to work produced by the residents of the *International Turning Exchange* and hosts a conference that explores various facets of the field from technical innovation to curatorial critique.

Curators' Focus: *Turning in Context* is the second major exhibition presented by the Berman Museum that explores the depth and variety of contemporary works of art created with the use of the lathe. Four curatorial voices provided the structure for the exhibition focus; artists were selected from around the globe for their vision, technique, and manipulation of the medium. Just as a bronze sculptor relies on the foundry and metalworking tools to produce a composition, a lathe-turning artist makes use of the lathe and metal or woodworking tools to orchestrate a creative vision. This exhibition seeks to explore how the lathe-turning field has evolved from having a purely decorative or functional orientation to incorporating dynamic sculptural forms with a message.

The partnership between the Berman Museum and the Wood Turning Center has expanded our knowledge and understanding of the art of lathe turning and we are pleased to have this opportunity to interpret and present this work to a larger audience. Our thanks to the staff and trustees of the Wood Turning Center for keeping this collaboration vital and fresh.

## *Curators' Focus*
## Acknowledgements

The Wood Turning Center is at a critical juncture in the evolution of lathe turning, and this exhibition could not have come into being without numerous dedicated people. We would first of all like to thank Stephen Hogbin and the Exhibition Committee of the Wood Turning Center for developing the concept used to design the *Curators' Focus* exhibition.

William Daley has had a long-term commitment to advancing the field of lathe turning, and our personal thanks go out for these years of service to the field and for his contribution to this catalog. We would like to extend our thanks and congratulations to the four curators who worked diligently and earnestly to construct an exhibition based on a complex and pluralistic vision of the turning field.

The Board of Trustees of the Wood Turning Center is pleased and honored to have the Winterthur Museum, Garden & Library as a collaborator in the *1997 World Turning Conference*. We extend our thanks to the staff of the Winterthur Museum for all that they have done to make the conference a success.

Our personal thanks go out to Lisa Tremper Barnes, Director of the Philip and Muriel Berman Museum, for her long-standing commitment to the turning field and for continuing the collaborative relationship between the Berman and the Wood Turning Center through this exhibition and conference.

The board and staff of the Wood Turning Center would also like to thank all of the generous foundations and individuals that contributed to the funding of this exhibition. The Windgate Charitable Foundation has been extremely supportive of this event through a challenge grant. The Arcadia Foundation, Penn State Industries, Pennsylvania Council for the Arts, the Pennsylvania Historical and Museum Commission, and the Philadelphia Cultural Fund all generously supported the conference and exhibition. Special thanks go out for all of the individual contributions made by friends and members of the Wood Turning Center.

Lastly, and most importantly, we want to express our sincere gratitude to all artist-turners for their extraordinary contributions to the field, and especially to those who submitted their work for consideration, whether or not it was included in this exhibition.

## *Curators' Focus*
## Introduction

Curators' Focus: *Turning in Context* is a major departure for the Wood Turning Center, which has sponsored a series of challenge exhibitions that invited artists to cast aside concern for market value and take creative risks by applying their personal aesthetics.

Drawing from Stephen Hogbin's "quadriform" idea of four aspects to turning creations — physical, emotional, spiritual, and intellectual — the Wood Turning Center evolved the current exhibition to be held in conjunction with the *1997 World Turning Conference: Turning Towards the 21st Century*.

As Lincoln Seitzman, a center trustee and member of the Exhibitions Committee, put it, Hogbin "proposed that we challenge the curators, rather than the artists, by assigning them each a different viewpoint from which to focus on the submitted work. When you select four respected people from art circles outside the wood turning field, ask them to select work, and ask them to write about their feelings for the work, it is not without risk."

More than 120 international artists submitted 350 entries to the curators' panel, which, applying their contextual viewpoints, selected 51 works by 39 artists. The artists, one quarter of whom are new to Wood Turning Center exhibitions, represent Australia, Canada, England, Germany, Italy, and the United States.

The four contextual aspects, and the curators who brought the "quadriform" ideas to bear on submissions, are:

- Physical context: materials and techniques, mind and muscle
  *Bruce Metcalf, a Philadelphia, Pennsylvania, jeweler/writer.*
- Emotional context: form, expression, and beauty
  *Maria van Kesteren, a Hilversum, the Netherlands, artist/turner.*
- Spiritual context: myths, icons, and beliefs
  *Mark Richard Leach, Curator of Twentieth Century Art at the Mint Museum of Art, Charlotte, North Carolina.*
- Intellectual context: issues and knowledge, mind and tool
  *David Revere McFadden, Executive Director of the Millicent Rogers Museum in Taos, New Mexico.*

In this volume, Stephen Hogbin presents his development of "quadriform" aspects, and the curators offer their essays on the aspects they applied to the submitted works. In addition, William P. Daley, Professor Emeritus of the Philadelphia University of Art and a ceramist and sculptor, tells about artists bringing "the 'how' of technology to form the 'why' of our spirits."

This catalogue is published on the occasion of the Curators' Focus: *Turning in Context* exhibition, Philip and Muriel Berman Museum of Art, Collegeville, Pennsylvania, September 25 through November 30, 1997, followed by a national tour from December 1997 through September 1999.

*Curators' Focus*
## Preface: Turning to the Culture of Memory

*Stephen Hogbin*

In the turning field, we often discuss the technical and the aesthetic — two criteria for working and thinking about our projects. A major interest in this exhibition is turning, or lathe work, along with experiencing the four aspects described here that can be found in most projects. Lathe work is a technique that creates form; form has a purpose. These aspects help the maker develop a conceptual relationship to the world.

For many years I have been interested in lists that consist of four aspects. For example, the four elements of earth, air, fire, and water; the four seasons; the Mandala; four directions; the cross in religion; or the simple X, a modest but powerful mark. In 1980 I wrote *Wood Turning: The Purpose of the Object*, which included a detailed quadriform I had evolved over ten years. I found a divergent growing awareness of the complexity of experience through a literary review of quadriforms.

The quadriform for this exhibition is one of the oldest from prehistory. More recently, through science's study of memory, another quadriform emerges. It is interesting to see how these two relate with a tantalizing loose fit. Through memory's subtle reconfiguration or inventive juxtaposition, we design and make our projects. In many ways it all seems rather obvious, while remaining elusive.

**Prehistory: Ancient Memories**

The oldest quadriform is from prehistory. It is the way we think our earliest ancestors organized their ideas about the universe. I have no doubt a good historian could identify when thinking got started. Was it the structure of the physical brain or the mental activity of the mind that developed patterns of thinking? *Homo sapiens* have been around for about one hundred and fifty million years — we have our traditions — and the structure of the brain seems like a place to collect some patterns of thinking and behavior. Carl Jung investigated mind patterns that relate to duoforms, triforms, quadriforms, mandalas, and schemata from diverse and ancient cultures. He also saw dreams and visions of contemporary people as archetypal patterns of thought somehow re-emerging from the deepest recess of the unconscious mind.

Earth, air, fire, and water was a quadriform that was used by early people to describe the major elements. Medieval thinkers and makers employed these elements in their symbolic designs.

## Vasari: The Artists' History

The next leap in time is to Giorgio Vasari closely followed by Johann Joachim Winckelmann. Vasari wrote *The Lives of the Artists* in 1568.[1] He is thought of as the first art theorist/historian who wrote about artists. He identified a process through which "Some men become great artists ...." This is relevant to the maker because it offers a theoretical basis for the activity and like any tool, it helps to get the required results or experience clarified. For Vasari some people became great artists through:

| | |
|---|---|
| application | physical |
| study | emotional |
| imitation | spiritual |
| knowledge of science | intellectual |

Knowing these four aspects will not of course make anybody a great artist but application does help. The quadriform can be part process and part category. Perhaps application is about craft and making. Study is about design, what has gone before, what is appropriate. Imitation for Vasari was about art and an accurate representation. The Renaissance was the time when representation of the visible world using perspective to control the image was a primary concern. What the retina sees is what the artist seeks to represent. Knowledge of the sciences speaks for itself. Artist and scientist were often synonymous in those times. Vasari's quadriform is rather category oriented, and it is necessary to wait almost two hundred years before Winckelmann presents it clearly as a procedure.

## Winckelmann: The History of Art

In 1764, Johann Joachim Wincklemann published the *History of Ancient Art*.[2] This was the first history of art. (Vasari had written the artists' history.) In the age of enlightenment Winckelmann's aim was to organize information rather than just chronicle it. This required an analytic tool of a different kind. Winckelmann's method of procedure "... involved the careful examination on the work of art." He included four steps:

| | |
|---|---|
| looking with the artist's eye | emotional |
| analyzing technical progress | physical |
| defining and identifying ideal beauty | spiritual |
| study of documentary evidence | intellectual |

1
**Bob Stocksdale**
Ebony Bowl, 1981
H 4" x Diam 7 1/4"
H 102 mm x Diam 184 mm
Ebony
Wood Turning Center Collection
L95.01.01.238

There is good reason to view a work analytically one step at a time. The difference between the Vasari and Winckelmann quadriforms is largely a matter of sequence and definition. If we think of the quadriform not as linear, but as something to be read simultaneously like a mandala, then it is quite a good fit. Some people maintain that the mind works like a hologram. The information is throughout the mind, stronger in one place than another, but connected and integrated. Also, one person may be very good at application and another at studying the documentary evidence — which part in the brain is stronger than another? Which muscle or group of muscles have been exercised? Occasionally there is the brilliance of the savant who excels in one particular way while remaining quite average in others.

In experiencing a Bob Stocksdale bowl [1], we can look and think about the four aspects that Wincklemann proposed. Looking with the artist's eye: the first part of a process of placing something in context of the visual experience. What is the form or design? What kind of shape is the bowl? Analyzing technical progress. How was it made? What techniques have been used to produce the bowl? What was it made from — the physical aspects. Defining and identifying ideal beauty. This is rather a hapless task and today it is approached differently. We think more of developing a conceptual relationship with a project. How do we think about and organize the piece into our experience? Really, this should be the last consideration if we are to think of it as a linear model. The study of documentary evidence may include any evidence that will help us construct a clearer understanding of the project. Who made it? Why was it made? What are the forms from the past that inform the project? I know that Stocksdale's work has been influenced by Japanese ceramics. To gain a further appreciation of his piece, I would need to look further at ceramic ware. This becomes a knowledge-based analysis much like the way a scientist would approach a project. We have gone through a process that reviews this project through the eyes and mind of the designer, craftsperson, artist, and scientist. Vasari and Winckelmann provide the foundation for much of how we approach the process of the project today. It also interests me how the Wincklemann quadriform overlaps with the exhibition quadriform.

| artist's eye | emotional | design |
| technical progress | physical | craft |
| ideal beauty | spiritual | art |
| evidence | intellectual | science |

**Fernie: A Contemporary Frame**

Eric Fernie, in *Art History and its Methods: A Critical Anthology*,[3] offers four aspects the project may convey, or categories in which we find objects:

| | |
|---|---|
| aesthetic and intellectual pleasure | spiritual |
| abstract form | emotional |
| social products | physical |
| expressions of cultures and ideologies | intellectual |

These aspects are generously inclusive, if a project can include all aspects, but Fernie admits some projects are valued more than others in certain places. Often if a project has a social purpose it will be relegated to an inferior strata. Public galleries have usually insisted that aesthetic and intellectual pleasure are a major defining aspect of quality. On occasion, skill in making has been disregarded or even intentionally shoddy, to avoid association with the hand, which is seen as inferior to the mind and conceptualization. Fernie holds that skill in making such as the "art of the silversmith" helps to reduce the distinction between art and craft. In the late twentieth century, art has been "characterized as a branch of philosophy practiced with materials and objects." This perception is held by a minority, and in other times and cultures we find other definitions of art. This quadriform is therefore less useful to makers than Fernie's investigatory form which he sees as overlapping approaches to the subject:

| | |
|---|---|
| investigation of available written documents | |
| investigation of the object using visual techniques | |
| investigation of social context | production and reception |
| construction or selection of system to relate to the object | ideologies and theories of art |

Fernie has presented categories in one quadriform and processes or methods of procedure in the other. The two are related. The process or sequence of investigation takes us through some categories. Makers are primarily concerned with processes, art historians primarily with the frame of categories. Eventually we each have to pay attention to each other's concerns. Vasari presented a mix of process and categories and Winckelmann presented a refined form of that mix and a clearer method of procedure. Skill and knowledge are active rather than passive. Makers will be drawn particularly to concepts that reinforce and refine activity because skill and procedure are their special knowledge. Process encourages learning and the development of new skills and information. Categories encourage memory and the persistence of learning. Most organisms can change in response to their experience and in a lifetime, the nervous system can be modified. Fernie has separated aspects of process and persistence but when we compare his second quadriform to that of Winckelmann and Vasari, there are striking similarities. Fernie's four investigations are not so different from those of Winckelmann's quadriform except the order has changed and the idea of beauty is advanced.

Our earliest ancestors were greatly influenced by the demands of the environment. Now we are influenced more by the demands of ideologies and theories of art. However, there are people who feel the tug of the environment and see the ideologies and theories that for example leave holes in the ozone, forests destroyed, etc., as reprehensible. I am concerned that for Fernie, the physical exists unequally in the rush for specialization and the specificity of intellectual inquiry. For many the physical is central or equally shared with the form and concept of the project. The demands of the environment, both natural and cultural, are essential aspects. The "wisdom of the elders" and the track record of some of the First Nation people who for thousands of years have lived in one place has directed my thinking about their quadriforms.

**Oakley: Human Evolution**

Next I have to leap into the twentieth century for a view of man's earliest beginnings. The essay by Kenneth P. Oakley, *Skill as a Human Possession*,[4] was suggested to me by Charles Hummel and leads us toward scientific inquiry and a framework from which to proceed. Oakley places the start of intelligence in the earliest tool-making activities of many birds and animals. Nests, beaver dams, and wasp burrows are an instinctive means of building for survival. Some of the instinctual activity may be learned by the young watching the activity of adults. Oakley explains how we moved from early primate instinctual behavior toward patterns of behavior that are learned. Most of the learning takes place in childhood and adolescence. I was about twelve when I first used a lathe, but it was only once and my skills were never fully developed. I still think that brief exposure was important to my later sustained interest. I never had the chance to work it through completely as a child — or maybe it's just coincidence.

2
**David Ellsworth**
Vessel, 1986
H 17" x Diam 17"
H 432 mm x Diam 432 mm
Broad-leaf maple burl
Collection of Lawrence and
Phyllis Sager

Visual acuity and skilled labor are also linked. Looking closely and intently does improve the ability to work with the other some of the time. Drawing from life is probably one of the best ways to develop skill in observation and possibly appreciation for the subject. The meditative concentration helps to focus the attention of not only the overall form but also the minute details. From that contemplation one hopes for an increased conceptual awareness. If the contemplation is concerned with the physical, the form's emotional implication, the spiritual connection, and intellectual potential, then a more rounded perception is developed. The eye, mind, and hand can then proceed in a balanced synchronicity. John Berger made an interesting observation on visual scrutiny and the response of the hand: "Once I started a drawing of her, just after she had been practicing. The piano was still open and she was sitting nearby. I screwed up my eyes and I waited. The impulse of a drawing comes from the hand rather than the eyes. Perhaps from the right arm, as with a marksman. Sometimes I think everything is a question of aim. Even playing Opus 110."[5]

Over time the hand developed from the apes' specialized ability to hang onto a branch to the human hand, which is now capable of so many dexterous operations. Big hands are just as dexterous as small hands; size does not seem to be entirely critical to skill. The changes that took place over millions of years have to be seen in relation to the whole organism. The eye, brain, and hand become a unit; lose one or the other and some skill becomes compromised. Oakley attempts to trace the origins of human behavior and points out that "Systematic making of weapons and tools could not follow until the cortex of the brain had attained a sufficient complexity of organisation." The complexity enabled conceptual thought and skilled behavior to have a close relationship. It is this relationship that still interests us today. In an age of automation and robots, why do we come together to study the 1,000-year-old technique of turning? You would think there is not much left to discover or even rediscover.

Tools have become very sophisticated compared to the chipped stone that formed the projectile point. Our interests have remained in the relationship of eye, mind, and hand. With all the new technologies, the crafts remain a site of integrated experience that empowers the individual at a physical, intellectual, emotional, and spiritual level. Any tool, like the computer, that takes over the relationship of eye, brain, and hand should be viewed with suspicion in the context of our interests. Conceptual thought for Oakley and its development is led by tradition coupled with invention. By developing the tradition, new concepts are formed. The artistic impulse is believed to have been present from earliest times, and that is one thing that has made us different from other animals, according to Oakley. Later he refers to it as pride in exercise of skill. *Homo sapiens* moved from hunters to cultivators and had time on their minds, which activated their hands to extend the vision of possibilities.

3
**Mark Lindquist**
Drum Song #1, 1987
H 23" x Diam 16 ½"
H 584 mm x Diam 419 mm
Walnut
Wood Turning Center Collection
L95.01.01.137

For Oakley, evolution of skill depends on four main factors:

| | |
|---|---|
| powers of sensory perception | spiritual |
| ability to coordinate sensory impressions, past and present | intellectual |
| physical capacity of the organism | physical |
| demands of the environment | emotional |

These factors are partly proactive and partly reactive to things such as the demands of the environment. This quadriform resonates with that of Vasari and Winckelmann even if it separates out the all-important conceptualizing ability of people. A loose structure seems to be in place from our very earliest evolutionary beginnings. It was the resonation between different quadriforms that made the form of so much interest to me. It became a puzzle of what the connection was about.

Last September, I came across an Associated Press article in the *Globe and Mail* titled "Study Supports Theory on Human Memory: Scientists Suspect Brain Has Four Systems That Handle Different Forms of Information."[6] This interested me because the brain is of course central to the patterns we experience, and it suggests a connection for me. Do all these quadriforms share the same pattern because the brain is structured in a very particular manner? Oakley does not actually make that connection, although in his essay the human brain is illustrated and central to the concept of skill.

**Piaget: Stages in Child Development**

Vasari comments on the development of the arts as having its own cycle bigger than the individual who is born, grows up, becomes old, and dies. For now the focus remains on the individual rather than the larger community even though comparisons will be drawn later. Categories, processes, and procedures have informed several quadriforms so far, and I was interested to compare Jean Piaget's four major stages in the development of the child.[7] They become a loose fit to what we have looked at so far.

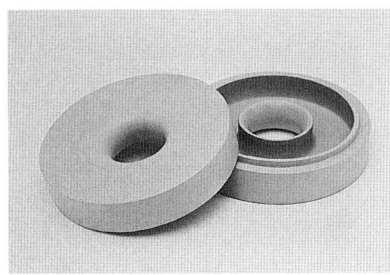

4
**Maria van Kesteren**
Box, 1987
H 2" x Diam 5 1/8"
H 51 mm x Diam 130 mm
Elm and gray paint
Wood Turning Center Collection
95.01.01.258

Piaget identified the four stages of mental development for children as:

    sensorimotor intelligence
    which covers the first two years of life        physical

    intuitive or symbolic thought
    which spans the preschool years        spiritual

    concrete operational thought
    of the seven and eight year old        emotional

    formal operations in early adolescence        intellectual

Sensorimotor intelligence develops through the child's own actions and perceptions on whatever surrounds it. Intuitive or symbolic thought develops language, mental images, and symbols that refer to the world. Concrete operational thought enables the child to see the world from another's perspective and is able to go between different modes of thought. Formal operations enables the adolescent to "perform mental actions upon symbols as well as on physical entities." Abilities develop and concepts can be manipulated and problems solved with relevant variables.

It is appropriate to look at the turning field to think about stages of development. In the last fifty years, starting with James Prestini, who made very simple bowls, we can see the evolution of what is an essentially physical object. It draws very little attention beyond its functional physical form. It is not charged with emotion and we have to wait until possibly Rude Osolnik or certainly David Ellsworth's large hollow vessels [2] to find emotional content in turned work. David Pye produced elegant bowls and lidded containers that were not charged with emotion but certainly carried a quality beyond just a physical presence. Mark Lindquist [3], through scale, pattern, an evocative use of the material, and a modernist iconography, presents the turning as a deeply personal spiritual search. Jim Partridge scorched and burned his turnings, giving them the aura of prehistoric ritual objects found by archeologists. Few have worked consistently in an intellectual manner in the turning field. Maria van Kesteren [4] is one of the few through an enigmatic minimalist aesthetic. Karen McCoy's *Sinkers and Swimmers* [5] is a recent project that stirred the debate. I have not seen the installation but it probably has to be experienced at a conceptual level or intellectual manner. Is the development I mention merely coincidence or does it have do with the maturation of contemporary turning? A difficult question to answer when we are still working on the solutions to the scope of the field. The boundaries of our field will, I hope, never be ultimately defined as a fence. I think we need to look elsewhere if we are to continue to grow as people.

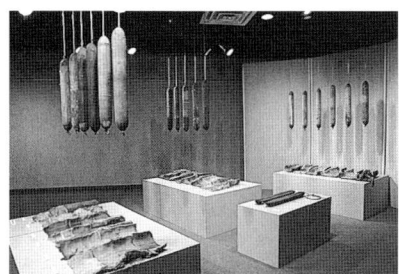

5
**Karen McCoy**
gallery installation of "Northern Project: Sinkers and Swimmers for Watson Creek, 1986"
Various woods, wool, and cotton
image Wood Turning Center Library

## Robbins: The Structure of Memory

It was an article about T.W. Robbins' research into Parkinson's disease[8] that catalyzed for me the potential that many quadriforms relate to the systems of memory. However, Robbins is tentative in specifying four systems. It is possible and perhaps probable that the quadriforms are all based on the structure of memory. Intuitively or possibly through systematic trial and error, the drawn quadriforms of the past represent repeating patterns of thought.

Memory can be stored in one or various parts of the brain. A simple memory will probably reside in one area, a complex memory in several. Each area will store the memory differently with each contributing in its own particular way. A simple fact as compared to a complex procedure will be stored separately and differently. Complexity of the experience is crucial to what goes where, how it gets there and how well it imprints. According to Larry R. Squire in *Memory and Brain*,[9] when something is learned, the context in which something is learned, and the relevance of what is learned all have an important bearing on memory.

A great demonstrator like Vic Wood or Dale Nish always has a story to tell that brings another dimension to the process. In subtle ways Vic Wood presents design theory through the story told and the action of demonstration, knowing that for some students there is enormous resistance to the ideas of design or an emotional component. Richard Raffan is also a master of this as demonstrated in his excellent book, *Turned-Bowl Design*.[10] While it is all miraculously connected in the intelligent and subtle mind, one kind of thinking and memory cannot entirely substitute for the other.

## A Full Circle

The physical, emotional, spiritual, and intellectual is a quadriform observed by Jung based on the First Nation sacred and symbolic structures. It is doubtful if the quadriform goes back one hundred and fifty million years, but how about a mere million? Perhaps the physical, emotional, spiritual, and intellectual are also stages in child development but I tend to think of them as contexts in which to work as an adult. Having learned and memorized these developments, it seems appropriate to continue exercising them. In our individual productions we will each excel in one more than another. It is probably true that the majority of turners in this exhibition are pretty good at the physical end of the project. What of the other contexts? I do not want to get into a simple cataloguing of complex experiences but at least I should show how I think it works.

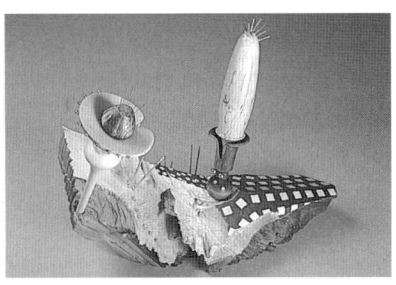

6
**Steve Loar**
Don't Stand So Close to Me,
1993 (Apr)
Mixed woods, beads, reeds,
acrylic paint, dye
H 14" x W 7" x D 8"
H 356 mm x W 178 mm x D 203 mm
image Wood Turning Center
Library

7
**Mark Sfirri**
Table, 1996
Curly maple, mahogany
H 20" x W 14" x D 19"
H 508 mm x W 356 mm x D 483 mm
Collection of Scott and Kate
Weymouth
image Wood Turning Center Library

Steve Loar [6] produces physical and emotional projects based in a storytelling tradition. The tradition is given an inventive flair through popular songs that inspire the form and content. Mark Sfirri's [7] ingenious off-center turning offers an intellectual challenge of how it was made. His projects combine a formal inquiry with occasional references to popular culture. The physical constraints of his particular technique have been elaborated imaginatively with style and wit. Robyn Horn and Frank Cummings both produce highly physical and spiritual projects. The iconography of Cummings' project draws us towards the human condition. Cummings says when referring to his project "… they enrich the soul and contribute to the spiritual and emotional well-being of the human condition." Horn's project is more relational, contrasting formal elements and juxtaposing a line to a circle in the context of an organic form. Merryll Saylan [8] has an intellectual edge to her practice based in the theory of design. Over the years her forms have developed and now have surfaces rich in color and texture. Saylan's approach has always been theoretical, although recently she has added a narrative or story-telling dimension to her new work. These observations are cursory and lacking the depth the individual projects and people deserve, but they should help position what I believe is the foundation for what is being produced.

Almost all mature work seems to cross the threshold of the physical, emotional, spiritual, and intellectual. I say almost because there has been some conceptual work that has attempted to specialize and reduce all the contexts except for one. I think this work is interesting but short lived and will be relegated to the storage areas in the not-too-distant future. To produce something that is physically well organized is difficult, and it requires considerable skill learned over time. But in the crafts, some of the physical can be learned fairly quickly, which is of course part of its attraction. Other projects take many hours of painstakingly deliberate and concentrated work. To create something fresh and original requires another leap that connects experience in new ways. To bring knowledge to a project that connects us to the rest of the world, to contexts other than materials and making, requires a highly agile nervous system. My point is that when these elements are compressed into one project with integrity you have a very powerful experience.

The four aspects should become a secondary shorthand compared to the complexity of the multilayered, multifaceted, multidimensional presence of the project. What each context means for each turner or person living with the work will vary enormously. Can you imagine reaching consensus on what is spiritual? But that is no reason not to use the word. I define the quadriform this way: For me spiritual is the sense of connection to a larger experience; science as a knowledge-based activity creates frameworks while recognizing how systems fit together. To paraphrase Claude Levi Strauss, scientists create events by means of structures — makers create structures by means of events. The emotion or expressive aspect gives the project force and conviction engaging the imagination.

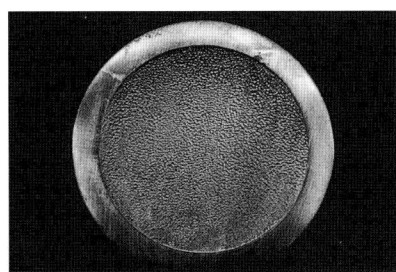

8
**Merryll Saylan**
North Seas, 1987
H 2 1/4" x Diam 20 1/2"
H 57 mm x Diam 521 mm
Maple, fiber-reactive dye, tung oil finish
Wood Turning Center Collection
95.01.01.212

The connections I have made between quadriforms are audacious, possibly sloppy, maybe brilliant, or perhaps are an overly simplistic formula for a highly complex situation that nobody has a grasp on. However, I think the quadriform is worth using as a guide to consider individual and collective progress. Like any physically effective form, it is worth contemplating in a spirit of criticality.

1  Eric Fernie, *Art History and its Methods: A Critical Anthology* (Phaidon Press, London, 1995).
2  Ibid.
3  Ibid.
4  Kenneth P. Oakley, "Skill as a Human Possession," in *A History of Technology:* Vol. 1 (Oxford at the Clarendon Press, Oxford, England, 1953).
5  Ibid.
6  Associated Press, "Study Supports Theory On Human Memory: Scientists Suspect Brain Has Four Systems that Handle Different Forms of Information," *Globe and Mail*, (Toronto, September 7, 1996).
7  Howard Gardner, *Art, Mind and Brain: A Cognitive Approach to Creativity* (Basic Books, New York, 1983).
8  Trevor W. Robbins, "Refining the Taxonomy of Memory," *Science* Vol. 273 (September 6, 1996).
9  Larry R. Squire, *Memory and Brain* (Oxford University Press, New York, 1987).
10 Richard Raffan, *Turned-Bowl Design* (Taunton Press, Newtown, Connecticut, 1987).

Stephen Hogbin is a sculptor, turner and author who lives in Wiarton, Canada. He was born in Tolworth, England in 1942.

Hogbin studied at Rycotewood College from 1957-58, and received a N.D.D. from Kingston College of Art, Kingston-Upon-Thames, England in 1961 and a Des. R.C.A from Royal College of Art, London, England in 1965.

Hogbin has lectured and written extensively, producing a monograph on his own work, *Wood Turning: The Purpose of the Object* and a retrospective catalogue, *Re: Turning, 1970-1990.*

His work has been represented in numerous exhibitions, among them, *Woodturning as a Fine Art: The Irving Lipton Collection*, at the Society for Arts and Crafts in Pittsburgh, Pennsylvania in 1992, *Conservation by Design*, Rhode Island School of Design in 1993, and *Challenge V: International Lathe-Turned Objects*, an exhibition that toured the USA from 1994-1997.

Hogbin's artwork is in public collections, including the Canadian Craft Museum, Vancouver, British Columbia, Canada, The Metropolitan Toronto Library, Canada, and the Wood Turning Center in Philadelphia, Pennsylvania.

# Notes On the Physical

*Bruce Metcalf*

Bruce Metcalf is a jeweler and writer who currently resides in Philadelphia, Pennsylvania. He was born in Amherst, Massachusetts on September 30, 1949.

Metcalf received a BFA from Syracuse University, New York in 1972 and a MFA from Tyler School of Art, Philadelphia, Pennsylvania in 1977.

He had solo exhibitions at the Susan Cummins Gallery, Mill Valley, California in 1994, Perimeter Gallery, Chicago, Illinois in 1993, and the United States Information Service Gallery in Seoul, Korea in 1990. His work was exhibited at the American Craft Museum, New York in 1992 and the Schmuckmuseum in Pfrozheim, Germany in 1989.

Metcalf's work can be seen in the collections of the Le Musee des Arts Decoratifs de Montreal, Canada and the Philadelphia Museum of Art, Pennsylvania.

He has received numerous awards and honors, including a Pew Fellowship in the Arts in 1996, a Fulbright Teaching/Research Fellowship to Korea in 1990 and National Endowment for the Arts Fellowships in 1977 and 1992.

I have been asked to write about the "physical context" of the work in this exhibition. This topic might include the quality of the material used, the tool employed in making the work, or the relationship between execution and design. To me, the most important aspect of the physical context of the objects in this exhibition is their craftsmanship: the way they were made and the degree of skill brought to bear in the making. Rather than survey the entire physical dimension of turning, I prefer to focus entirely on this one issue.

I'm a practicing craftsman, although I am not a wood turner. My work is generally well made, and I have a special fondness for superior craftsmanship. I love certain objects in which extraordinary workmanship is intrinsic to their character: Rene Thalique's jewelry, Henning Koppel's amazing pitchers and serving dishes for Georg Jensen, Yixing ceramic ware, Edo-period theatrical costumes and sword guards from Japan, and fine ship models. But my passion for fine craftsmanship must wrestle with my cooler, more intellectual appraisal of craft in general: There are lots of objects that are well-made, but not very good otherwise. I can think of herds of silver teapots made by well-meaning Americans in the 1950s that succeeded only in being pale imitations of Scandinavian work. Or furniture that takes bits and pieces from three or four historical styles, but fails to become anything more than a clumsy pastiche. If craftsmanship alone cannot make an object good, what am I to think of it?

In my role of juror of this exhibition, I was called upon to make very specific value judgments. Was the object we were looking at good enough to include in the exhibition or not? Was it a quality object? Most of the objects we reviewed were well made, so good craftsmanship was effectively a foregone conclusion. And yet, we rejected many objects that were well made. Why? Because we were implicitly asked to hold the work to a more complex standard: We were asked to consider these turned objects, at least in part, as art. The business of regarding an object as partly craft, and partly art, is a minefield of contradictions and pitfalls. The idea of craftsmanship is right there in the middle of that minefield, and that's the issue I'd like to examine here. What's the connection between fine craftsmanship and aesthetic quality?

The question of technique, and whatever it has to do with quality, is especially important to the field of turning. Here is a category of craft that is completely defined by technique. Material and function have no necessary connection to the definition of a turning. (Even though a conservative idea of "turning" might have initially denoted turned wooden bowls, by definition it must also include diverse materials like metals and plastics, and diverse forms like architectural embellishments and sculptures.) By defining the field, and by sponsoring exhibitions such as this one, an implicit value judgment has been made.

The difficulty of connecting technique and quality is not new. John Ruskin, in his 1849 *Seven Lamps of Architecture*, presents a typically assertive solution through "modes of admiration" of architecture. He mentions Sentimental Admiration, Proud Admiration, Artistic and Rational Admiration, and Workmanly Admiration. The last he defines as:

"The delight of seeing good and neat masonry, together with that belonging to incipient developments of taste, as, for instance, a perception of proportion in lines, masses, and moldings."

It's clear that he is talking about the admiration of good craftsmanship and good basic design in building. But he then proceeds to dismiss this type of pleasure:

"This, of course, though right within certain limits, is wholly uncritical, being as easily satisfied with the worst as with the best building, so that the mortar be laid smoothly. As to the feeling with which it is usually united, namely, a delight in the intelligent observance of the proportions of masses, it is good in all the affairs of life. But it no more constitutes the true power of an architect, than the possession of a good ear for metre constitutes a poet ..."

Ruskin then goes on to insist that Artistic and Rational Admiration is the only legitimate type of appreciation allowed. To Ruskin, fine workmanship counts for next to nothing. But there is a context here, and Ruskin was specifically addressing the condition of building in the mid-nineteenth century, when the many crafts of constructing and decorating buildings were still alive and well. Ruskin could assume good craftsmanship in almost every case: what he was doing was contrasting well-made but sterile Neo-classical architecture with rough but vital Gothic architecture. To Ruskin, a Corinthian capital could be exquisitely finished, but it couldn't hold a candle to the frequently clunky but inventive carvings of the Gothic.

Ruskin outlines a debate that continues to this day, and many people still don't agree with him. From one point of view (not Ruskin's), technique offers an objectively observable criterion of quality. If something is well made, it is good. Each craft offers a menu of craftsmanship points, which can be determined in a fairly straightforward manner. In wood turning, people look for absence of screw-holes in the bottom of the form, an even surface without scuffs and torn grain, and for thinness. Beyond this list of baseline accomplishments, one then looks for evidence of technical difficulty (a point to which I will return). The object that achieves the maximum amount of difficulty would then be the best object.

In this system, the ambiguities that plague Western aesthetics disappear. Quality is measurable. All the debates about aesthetic quality are useless, because an informed observer can tell how well a piece is made. In fact, there is a branch of the craft world that happily accepts this system: the world of replication. Each craft field has a segment which is entirely satisfied to repeat the accomplishments of the past, from replicas of Colonial furniture to reproductions of celadon pottery. A "good" object would be a perfect imitation of a known prototype, as long as the technique is difficult. The same standard of observable craftsmanship is also applied in scale model making.

Really good technique is often visible only to those who have firsthand knowledge about the craft. While some aspects of good craftsmanship, like a polished surface on a stone carving, are visible to almost anyone, most aspects are not so obvious. One must be an initiate, so to speak, to recognize these signs of skill. There is an aspect of craft that is a secret knowledge, revealed only to those who take the time and trouble to either learn firsthand, or to be taught by someone else who knows. For instance, a good handcut dovetail looks much like a dovetail made with a router and a jig: neither joint will show any space between the knuckles. However, the handcut dovetail must be carefully and laboriously sawed out, and the closeness of fit is testimony to the patience and skill of the woodworker. Only those who have intimate experience with both types of joint making will really know how difficult the hand process is, and how comparatively easy the routed dovetail is. Furthermore, the trained woodworker will be able to recognize the differences in size and spacing between a handmade and a routed dovetail joint, whereas most other observers will miss the distinction entirely. And so it is with many other points of great skill in craftwork: the perfectly planished surface in silversmithing; the thrown ceramic vessel with walls only a few millimeters thick; the perfectly straight selvage of a weaving. You could say that being able to recognize certain points of skill constitutes an initiation into the culture of craft.

The problem, as Ruskin pointed out, is that equating good technique with overall "goodness" remains almost wholly innocent of inspiration, inventiveness, or even of good design. In the end, I think this is a cultural issue: there is a segment of craft culture that values sheer craftsmanship above all other virtues, and correspondingly devalues creativity. Like many cultural phenomena, it cannot be proven that this value is intrinsically inferior or superior to any other. It simply exists, and the good people who believe in the value of technique have every right to do so.

However, equating fine craftsmanship with quality loses credibility once craft has aspirations to the status of art. The contemporary art world values inventiveness, ambition, historical awareness, and a type of philosophic discourse, at the same time that it tends to devalue craftsmanship. This is a fact, against which it is fruitless to protest. The historical reasons for this condition are complicated, but in the end, you have a powerful culture that devalues technique. And since it is clear that the ambition of this exhibition, as well as of the Wood Turning Center, is to promote turning to the level of art, the values of the art world must be taken into consideration. Of course, the moment you propose art world values as a measuring-stick for craft objects, you invite a bitter clash of cultures. And much of this clash centers around issues of technique.

It's now commonplace in the art academy to insist that a real artist is primarily invested in ideas, and that all other priorities must be secondary. In this world, the signifier of "artness" is the conceptual component of art. One of the widely accepted accounts for the centrality of art-as-concept is Arthur Danto's thesis that art is embodied meaning. Here, art is not so much an object, as it is a manipulation of idea. And, of course, Danto is probably right, when you consider that urinals, imitation Brillo boxes, and smearing one's naked body with chocolate have all come to be regarded as art. What else do such disparate phenomena have in common? The only thread that holds them all together is that they address an idea.

In the art academy, Danto's thesis gets distorted into a series of rules and regulations. One of these rules is that the artist should feel free to adopt or abandon any technique, just as long as the technique serves the concept. Measured against this value system, rigorous training in and loyalty to a specific medium fall short. Indeed, loyalty and mastery are frequently regarded as deeply suspect, and perhaps as proof of mental deficiency. Thus, these important craft-culture values stimulate deep suspicion in the art world.

In the craft world, things are different. Even though most craft practitioners won't say that good technique is the only criterion for quality, they remain deeply invested in their skills and their medium. Not by accident do people refer to themselves as "potters," "weavers," "woodworkers," and the like. Each of these terms suggests an apprenticeship to the demands of a material and its processes, none of which can be learned quickly and easily.

Those who learn a craft understand what constitutes mastery. This is a tricky concept, because it is mixed up with the art world concept of the "masterpiece." Supposedly, the masterpiece is a great work of art in which not one single element could be changed without diminishing it. Luckily, this idea has lost favor, because it has become clear that our ideas of what constitutes greatness can change greatly over time. But it turns out that the art world borrowed the "masterpiece" business from the crafts. At one time, the masterpiece was an object made by a journeyman to prove his skill, and thus to become a master. The guilds closely controlled this status, because it carried with it such privileges as being able to operate one's own shop, to take apprentices, and to be able to sell certain types of merchandise. The masterpiece was a ticket to prosperity — but it was often an extraordinary object in its own right.

For instance, consider the masterpiece once required of a Danish silversmith. Starting with a disc of flat metal, the journeyman smith first had to hammer up a perfectly smooth sphere, of a specified size, with a round opening at the top. A review board would examine the sphere, carefully testing it for any surface variations. Then the smith would have to hammer the sphere back into a six-pointed cross, with each arm perfectly straight and square in section. The board would again examine the object, testing it for uniformity. If the piece was perfect, the journeyman became a master. Anyone who has ever tried to raise a piece of metal into a hollow form can tell you how incredibly difficult this would be. To the best of my knowledge, nobody in this country has done this in the last 50 years. The degree of experience, practice, and technical skill required is beyond most Americans, myself included.

But the masterpiece is not just an object, or a record of technical skill, or a ticket to prosperity. It is also testimony to having completed a long and difficult process. That is to say, mastery is not just skill, but an indication of the craftsman's character.

The training required to achieve a high degree of skill demands patience, perseverance, and a rigorous attention to detail. These are moral qualities: elements of character. While we might belittle the idea of good character, it's also clear that we look for a such a person when the chips are down. If we are faced with a difficult situation and need assistance, whether we need a plumber or a lawyer, we look for exactly these aspects of character. We want someone who will work carefully, someone who can see the job through to the end, and someone who pays attention to the details. It is precisely these qualities that technical mastery requires. Seen in this light, the well-crafted object shows evidence of its maker's experience and moral character.

In the Western discourse about art, the biographical aspects of the maker are not afforded much respect (unless you're a novelist, playing up the suffering of Van Gogh or Michelangelo). Until recently, art theory demanded that the audience regard the art object as an isolated phenomenon, so better to experience aesthetic pleasure. Postmodern theory threw strict isolation out the window, so that the artwork's reception could be examined within a social context. The postmodern critic will discuss the artwork not just as an isolated object on a pedestal, but as a contribution to ongoing social process. However, if the context of the artwork becomes a legitimate subject for inquiry, why shouldn't we consider the experience of the maker? I would assert that craft and craftsmanship point directly to the maker, and, in fact, you don't fully comprehend craft unless you consider the moral and experiential component of its production. Skill and loyalty to a medium are not artistic failings, but moral strengths.

So, what does all this mean when applied to real objects?

Consider William Hunter's *Dalbergia Cyclone* [1], one of my favorite objects in this exhibition. It's clear that Hunter has been practicing his craft for some time (since at least 1969, he says), for the resolution between design and technique is about as close to perfect as you can get. While the technique might be difficult, Hunter does not push it to the foreground. Instead, he gives priority to the complex visual play of mass and void, and to the sheer beauty of figured wood. The profile, which is probably rooted in Chinese ceramics, is simple and elegant.

But you can also "see through" the object, to the years of practice, experimentation, and failure that Hunter endured before he could arrive at this point. And all that practice is meaningful: how many people today are capable of such sustained discipline? Not too many, I would venture. The object is testimony to a man's good character.

So Ruskin's "Workmanly Admiration" has more substance than he admitted. What remains to be contested is whether *Dalbergia Cyclone* is art or not. Personally, I don't think so. However, I also don't think the inability to achieve the status of art is actually a failure. To me, *Dalbergia Cyclone* places itself in the long and admirable history of craft objects, intended to bring pleasure to its audience and warmth to the interior space where it eventually will be seen. It is a great piece of decorative art, and there should be no shame in that. The literary and philosophical demands placed upon a work of art are not terribly appropriate here. The context of decorative art is different than the context of art, as are the cultures they spring from. This is plainly not a work of conceptual art. It's equally obvious that this is an object rooted in craft culture, with its respect for sheer physical skill. Sometimes art world values can just go to hell: *Dalbergia Cyclone* is an excellent piece of craft and a fine piece of decorative art. And the way it was made — the full range of implications about how it was crafted — contribute greatly to its quality.

1
**William Hunter**
Dalbergia Cyclone, 1995
H 6" x W 11" x D 11"
H 152 mm x W 279 mm x D 279 mm
Cocobolo rosewood
collection of Ruth and David Waterbury

## *Fascination for the Circle:*
## Form, Expression, and Beauty

*Maria van Kesteren*

Maria van Kesteren is a lathe-turning artist who lives and works in Hilversum, the Netherlands. She was born on August 22, 1933.

van Kesteren's work has been exhibited in galleries and museums around the world, including: the Crafts Council, London, England in 1992, Galerie Binnen, Amsterdam, the Netherlands in 1993, *Made in Holland, Design aus den Niederlanden*, at the Museum fur Angewandte Kunst, Cologne, Germany in 1994, *Retrospective from 1960*, Stedelijik Museum, Amsterdam in 1995, and the *Dutch Jewelry Touring Exhibition* which traveled throughout Indonesia in 1995.

Examples of van Kesteren's work are included in the collections of the Cooper-Hewitt Museum, New York, Municipal Gallery of Modern Art, Dublin, Ireland, Museum fur Kunsthandwerk, Frankfurt, Germany, Stedelijik Museum, Amsterdam, the Netherlands, and the Wood Turning Center, Philadelphia, Pennsylvania. Her work is also in numerous private art collections around the world.

The theme of this exhibition and conference indicates that the material of which the object was made is not essential, but, indeed, more important is the forming process of turning. In this exposition there will be objects not only made of wood but also of metal and alabaster.

The title, *Turning in Context*, that marks this exhibition organized by the Wood Turning Center in Philadelphia also expresses the lines along which I can enthusiastically identify myself as a curator and a wood turner.

The restrictive and limiting framework of material or medium will thus be purposefully broken so that the shape becomes prominent. Referring to an exhibition of my work in 1981, I expressed myself as follows:

"... In my work I am concentrated on and motivated to develop round forms in their limitless variations ... quite secondary to this is the fact that I use wood as a medium."

Although I sympathize with the material wood, I am not limited by it, and so I work also in glass and perspex. As one of the four members of the jury, I chose to review the competitive pieces from the standpoint of Emotional Context referring to Form, Expression and Beauty.

To me, as a curator, the primary context is emotional and the other contexts — physical, spiritual and intellectual — are subordinated to the emotional. If and when an object touches me emotionally, then I can take the other contexts (subcontexts in my opinion) into consideration.

In my experience, it is often difficult or impossible to see the aesthetic value of an object through the spiritual veil.

1
**Merryll Saylan**
Turning 60, I:18
(work in progress), 1996
Maple
H 8" x W 26" x D 16"
H 203 mm x W 660 mm x D 406 mm
lent by the artist

The intellectual context appeals to me insofar as I consider and admire the means to obtain harmony, simplicity and restrained tension in lathe turning. To be frank, I do not appreciate the artificial and affected aspects in artistic expression. Physical context is inferior to form and expression.

For me, an object's first impression has to be surprising, consistent and refreshing, but above all convincing and inevitable. Only after all that do materials and techniques count.

In spite of striving for objectivity, every jury member cannot escape his or her own subjectivity on taste and philosophy. Since I am an artist too, all my artistic actions will inevitably color my affinities and restraints.

**Fascination for the Circle**

The circle is a form burdened with symbols in many cultures throughout the ages.

Many phrases and sayings derive their natural strength from the circle. The round form is more organic and more archetypal than the square form, the polygon and the triangle.

A circle simply exists, while a polygon is a secondary form made through external actions. In this sense, a square is something constructed and a circle something organic. By turning, one never can escape the circle, the round form. Sometimes the circle demoralizes you by its mathematics and inevitability; all forms that one wants to express derive from and lead back to the circle.

The circle dares you: you can attack its perfect round form by creating another circle; you can confront it by confronting it with itself.

1
**Robin Wood**
Nest of Pole-Lathe Turned Bowls,
1995
H 5" x Diam 13"
H 125 mm x Diam 325 mm
Spalted beech
lent by the artist

There are also moments that the circle gives one deep satisfaction, because one is able to break through the seeming limitation and unassailability; the circle reveals itself by repeatedly new transformations.

In my opinion there are two ways to give direction to working from the circle:

The first takes the introverted way, where one respects the circle as a form and where the circle is provoked by the turning process to multifarious round forms. One chooses to stay within the cadres of the round form and one hopes that "Im der Beschraenkung der Meister sich zeigt," [Through limitations the master reveals himself].

This way can lead to intimacy, internalization and deepening of the form. But this road also can be a dead-end paved with superficial, soulless and superfluous circular constructions that respect the form but only as a dead form without transformation into new life.

The second way is the extroverted road. The in-itself perfect circle form challenges the artist into a more aggressive approach whereby the perfection is fallen upon: the artist attacks the circular form.

This battle can present very thrilling and surprising results, where a spectator can go through the same thrills that originate in the final object between the circle forming and outward circle forming elements. Through all the stages of workmanship, the circular form as a start and inspiration can still be identified.

Although in the worst case, something impudent and spectacular has been created; it is fundamentally soulless. Spectacular structure, decorations and maybe technical heights can block the development of a pure and convincing design, that in my opinion originates in the turning form, the round form.

It appears to be obvious to start from ceramic forms: cups, vases and, in general, objects of a constant thickness. In ceramics, this is almost a necessity because otherwise the danger exists of irreparable damage during the baking process. Technical freedom is much greater with wood turning.

There is a fundamental difference in the nature of the material for lathe turning and ceramics. Wood is not an amorphous material but has — as an element — its own form. Therefore, the wood turner only can remove material, while the ceramist — starting from a formless lump of clay — only can add to it. The wood turner, like the sculptor, is involved in an irreversible process, while the ceramist can turn back on a once-taken road: a reversible process. This is of essential importance for the decisions made during the creation process.

The wood turner can create a piece of art that harmonizes 100 percent with the notion he or she had in mind, only if every decision he or she makes along the way goes in the right direction. His or her concentration must be a bent bow from the beginning to the end.

The use of wood has a very long tradition. As early as prehistory, the first people could apply primitive stone tools to simple woodworking, for example to create defensive weapons and simple utensils. Through the centuries, wood has remained one of the most important materials used to make tools and art objects. By the emanation of wood as a living material it is close to man by its structure, color and touchability. Even treatment of the surface is seldom strictly necessary.

**Wood Guarantees Easy Results and Response**

Since the discovery of the wheel there has been a need to create circular objects. The lathe is therefore an ideal tool. Although the lathe for industrial purposes has surpassed the wood lathe, the latter continues to be a convenient tool because of its simple construction and use.

2
**Ernst Gamperl**
Bowl, 1996
H 5 ¾" x Diam 7 ⅛"
H 145 mm x Diam 180 mm
African ebony
lent by the artist

2
**Mike Shuler**
Gabon Ebony Bowl #818, 1996
H 5" x Diam 12 1/8"
H 127 mm x Diam 306 mm
Gabon ebony, choc-te-kok,
cocobolo, Brazilian tulipwood,
goncalo alves
lent by the artist

The artist, often not technically educated and in search of new expressions, uses these characteristics to give birth to his ideas. Besides pure turning, the lathe can play a role in adding shapes to not-round forms. This exhibit contains many examples. In my work I seldom feel the need to add treatments of the wood.

The wood turner is exposed to certain temptations inspired on the one hand by the technique and on the other hand by the material. Both cloud the vision of the artist about his object.

Because turning as an industrial process has become one of the most important removable treatments, many tools have developed in this field to make turning more efficient and economical. A one-way traffic arose from the industry of technical achievements such as tools and accessories.

The wood turner who might not be satisfied with his objects will find it tempting to enlarge in his instruments, thinking that ideas will eventually come. Lots of wood turners look in this direction. Seldom is the result convincing.

The exterior features of the material (grain, capricious markings, knots, burls, holes) attract lots of people, and tempt one to think that a spectacular piece of wood needs hardly any adding. The reality is the contrary: the state of the surface distracts from the form.

To give the form its optimal tension, it is often better to suppress the natural color and markings by adding a coating or by starting out with a kind of wood as neutral as possible, for example lime or maple.

### The Curators

For decades there has been a clear shifting from applied art to autonomous art. This stretching of bounds exists in one way because artists make use of the most various materials and techniques.

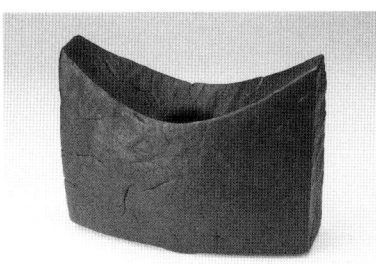

3
**Jim Partridge**
Hard Mouthed Spode Form, 1996
H 8" x W 8" x D 4"
H 203 mm x W 203 mm x D 101 mm
Scorched burr oak
lent by the artist

3
**Melvyn Firmager**
Seaflower #340, 1996
H 4 1/2" x Diam 5"
H 114 mm x Diam 127 mm
Ebonized eucalyptus gunnii
lent by Dr. Irving Lipton

On the other hand, handicraftsmen consciously choose this type of art. For a group exhibition like this one, it is necessary that pictures of the artists' work are judged. These photographs or slides often do not do justice to the originals. They are never able to show the obvious existence to which they are entitled by the artist's creativity. Also the quality of the pictures differ. The members of the jury examined the slides of the work of about 200 artists and made a selection.

In order to get more insight into the diversities of the selected work, I have catalogued the objects. This classification doesn't pretend to be more than a helpful survey.

In the first instance it is a personal encounter between visitor and objects.

**Categories of Turned Forms**

1. Objects that join tradition and handicraft next to personal design. In contrast to the choices of *Challenge V*, this jury chose to include simple objects, such as bowls, cups and boxes.[1]

2. Turned objects that — apart from design — were affected by such techniques as gougings, inlay and coloring.[2]

3. The deformation of round turned-forms by burning and using wet wood or by sawing and joining (with the emphasis on the construction).[3]

4. Objects that are connected with three dimensional art (primarily one's own personal feelings and experiences).[4]

These categories answer the expectations of the theme "Turning in Context." A possible interpretation of this theme is: "Turned work matched into non-turned work."

Emotional Context   *31*

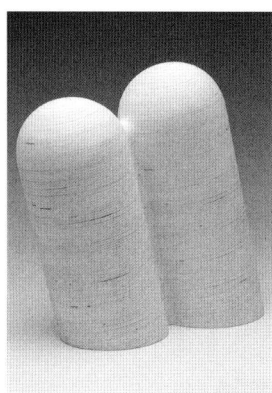

4
**Richard Hooper**
White Bipod, 1995
H 14" x W 14" x D 5"
H 355 mm x W 355 mm x D 127 mm
Birch ply
lent by the artist

Of the above mentioned categories, numbers 3 and 4 fit the chosen theme best because these objects have undergone some other treatments besides turning. Not everything is round.

We hoped that artists of other disciplines would be attracted by the wider interpretation of turning. This expectation was not realized completely. Exceptions are the objects of metal. The personal and surprising results in this hard material showed a freer interpretation of the theme.

To be clear: the jury has not judged the selection by the categories but has evaluated and appreciated every object on its own.

Within the selection I was disappointed that so few artists make boxes. Especially because the box gives one freedom to express: to create a tension between open and closed, between in and out, between spontaneity and reserve, between openness and disguise.

Furthermore, the box is a constant invitation: it calls "touch" and "feel," but also requires respect for its own encircled privacy (intimacy). In expositions, one often sees people caressing and touching the objects as if they have a tactile attraction.

In 1960 I started my own studio. The self-chosen limitations of the turned form, have challenged me on every occasion to discover new thematics. These considerations form the credo of my work as an artist and as a member of this jury. With these I justify all my artistic and judging activities.

4
**Helen Shirk**
Sustaining Spirit VIII, 1994
H 7" x W 20" x D 20"
H 177 mm x W 508 mm x D 508 mm
Copper, patina, prismacolor
lent by the artist

1  *Turning 60, I:18 (work in progress)* by Merryll Saylan and *Nest of Pole-Lathe Turned Bowls* by Robin Wood

2  *Bowl* by Ernst Gamperl and *Gabon Ebony Bowl #818* by Mike Shuler

3  *Hard Mouthed Spode Forms* by Jim Partridge and *Seaflower #340* by Melvyn Firmager

4  *White Bipod* by Richard Hooper and *Sustaining Spirit VIII* by Helen Shirk

# Myths, Icons, and Beliefs

*Mark Richard Leach*

Mark Richard Leach is the Curator of Twentieth Century Art at the Mint Museum of Art in Charlotte, North Carolina. He was born on February 6, 1954. Leach received a BA from the University of Arkansas at Little Rock, College of Fine Art in 1981 and an EdM in Twentieth Century Art and Non-profit Administration Education from Harvard University, Boston, Massachusetts in 1987.

Leach has curated many exhibitions for the Mint Museum, such as *Michael Lucero: Sculpture 1976-1994* in 1996, *Recollections: Lumbee Heritage* in 1995, and *ARTCurrents 6: Material Redemptions* in 1991. He co-curated *Revolving Techniques: Clay, Glass, Metal, and Wood* with Albert LeCoff for the Mitchener Art Museum in Doylestown, Pennsylvania.

His writings include: *Signs of Support: Furniture Forms in Contemporary American Art*, Design West: 79-80, *Tarleton Blackwell*, New Art Examiner, *Shared Vision or Dueling Agendas? Curators on Excellence and Equity* in the AAM Excellence and Equity Newsletter, and *Michael Lucero: Sculpture 1976 -1994*.

"... And there are those who regret that with the improvements of cultivation the sublimity of the wilderness should pass away; for those scenes of solitude from which the hand of nature has never been lifted, affect the mind with a more deep toned emotion than ought which the hand of man has touched. Amid them the consequent associations are of God the creator — they are his undefiled works, and the mind is cast into contemplation of eternal things."[1]

Thomas Cole, 1835

Forests and the trees they comprise have, for centuries, symbolized a great many things to humans. To say that before the industrial period there existed a symbiotic relationship between humanity and nature would be an overstatement. Nevertheless, for many indigenous societies, nature was a respected partner.

On the North American continent, especially in the nineteenth century, the pictures of Remington, Bierstadt, Church, Moran, and a good many others, seized nature's splendor, tranquillity, and mercurial disposition. If only in a rudimentary way, such observed phenomena contained the suggestion of an even more powerful idea, that of the spiritual. According to artist Thomas Cole, "It was not that the jagged precipices were lofty, that the encircling woods were of the dimmest shade, or that the waters were profoundly deep; but that over all, rocks, wood, and water, brooded the spirit of repose, and the silent energy of nature stirred the soul to its inmost depths."[2]

Evidence of our desire to attain spiritual fulfillment through nature can be found in unlikely places. For example, though made for children, the Walt Disney motion picture Pocahontas was made by adults. Educational and entertaining, one of the film's narratives nonetheless, is the personification of the spiritual in nature. Grandmother Willow, one of the film's principal characters, who is also a tree, is a gentle and maternal forest elder who dispenses the wisdom of the ages. Arguably enchanting,

1
**Christian Burchard**
Dance, 1996
H 6" x W 6" x D 6 ¼"
H 152 mm x W 152 mm x D158 mm
Osage orange, paint
lent by the artist

the idea that trees can talk in the literal sense isn't the film's message. Rather, a different reading might be that by "listening" to nature, we can hear ourselves. If we are open to hand-made objects, they can promote, albeit indirectly, re-engagement with nature, self, and the eternal.

Though objects may be catalysts for spiritual epiphanies, what might the notion of spirituality mean to the wood turner and how might such ideas be manifest in the finished object? At best, such meditations are speculative in the larger sense. However, artists included here have indicated their affinity with spiritual ideas and it is through the information submitted by them that our inquiry will be conducted.

Wood can possess many qualities and those perhaps least or seldom considered turn upon notions of the eternal. Forests can offer us a connection to the past in a way no other living species can. For those who can interpret it, the trunk of a tree is encrypted with numerous kinds of information. Geography, soil minerals, light conditions, and much more also contribute to the formative character of trees. Different tree specimens react to and are fed by such conditions in altogether unique ways. Such phenomena imbue pieces of timber with qualities both desired and, sometimes, a hindrance to the execution of a turned piece or to the overall appearance of the end result. Wood grain, occlusions, and spalting can be used by turners in much the same way painters use color and brush stroke to distinguish surface, even to convey ideas. But unlike moments of time that pass and cannot be retrieved, nature's ephemerality is transformed into perpetual record in the marks which trees contain. It is this sense of permanence that some associate with or understand metaphorically to connote notions of the eternal. Such potentially superficial qualities can, if viewed in the context of living things and history, provoke what some might describe as transcendent experiences.

Wood turners can combine seemingly unrelated conceptual and technical vectors to reveal particular ideas, even suggest aspects of the spiritual. Among the artists for whom the eternal or the universal are

2
**Melvyn Firmager**
Seaflower #340, 1996
H 4 ½" x Diam 5"
H 114 mm x Diam 127 mm
Ebonized eucalyptus gunnii
lent by Dr. Irving Lipton

Spiritual Context

3
**William Hunter**
Dalbergia Cyclone, 1995
H 6" x W 11" x D 11"
H 152 mm x W 279 mm x D 279 mm
Cocobolo rosewood
lent by Ruth and David Waterbury

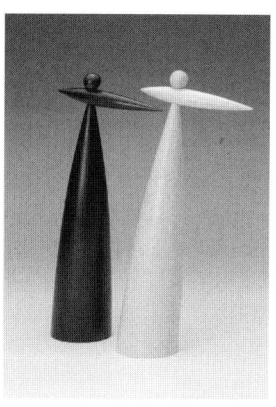

4
**William Leete**
Pepper & Salt Mills, 1996
Each H 10 1/2" x W 4 1/2" x D 2 1/2"
H 266 mm x W 114 mm x D 63 mm
Walnut, maple, steel, dye,
bleach, wax, paint, sealer, epoxy
lent by the artist

meaningful in their works, the manifestations of this subject are expressed using several vehicles. Some (Burchard, Firmager, Hunter, Leete, Moulthrop, and Shirk) speak of the vessel as a spiritual container. There are several (Hooper, McKay, Peteran, and Shuler) for whom abstraction offers the potential to speak of such ideas. And for others (Saylan and Wood), technique and the ritual of execution provide avenues to engage these ideas. On occasion, the above artists cross between the outlined areas.

### The Vessel

Vessels are frequently described as receptacles, and for some of the artists included here this notion becomes a factor in expressing concerns for the spiritual. For example, Christian Burchard's *Dance* [1] is both a vessel and a simple sphere. According to the artist, he sees the "... Vessel as a container of spirit."[3] His vessel's highly finished surface becomes a dramatic backdrop for the activated gestures scored into its surface. The trajectory and directness of the surface markings imply a perpetual phenomenon like subatomic particles orbiting a nucleus.

Melvyn Firmager believes that the vessel is "... Symbolic of where we came from, our spirituality, the goddess within."[4] His *Seaflower* [2] is a vital, animated container, whose undulating manifold is the by-product of the artist's collaboration with the material. Firmager uses wood that is regarded by most as unusable because it is unstable. His interest in process and unstable material, particularly from a conceptual viewpoint, finds a parallel in Soetsu Yanagi's description of a chance encounter with Korean lathe-turning:

"I noticed at once by their workshop many big blocks of pine wood ready for the hand lathe. But to my astonishment, all of them were still sap green and were by no means ready for immediate use. ... A Korean craftsman took one of them, set it in a lathe, and began forthwith to turn it. The pine block was so fresh that turning made a wet spray, which gave off a scent of resin. ... I asked the artisan, 'Why do you use such green material? Cracks will come out pretty soon.'

" 'What does it matter?' was the calm answer. I was amazed by this Zen monklike response. I felt sweat on my forehead. Yet I dared to ask him, 'How can you use something that leaks?' 'Just mend it,' was his simple answer.

"With amazement I discovered that they mend them so artistically and beautifully that the cracked piece seems better than the perfect one. So they do not mind whether it cracks or not. ...They live in a world of 'thusness,' not of 'must or must not.' Their way of making things is so natural that any man-made rule becomes meaningless."[5]

Thus Firmager's and the Korean wood turner's results might be best described as harmonious settlements in which artistic vision, adaptive approach, and fluid technique commune with and embrace nature's inherent uncertainty.

About *Dalbergia Cyclone*, [3] "The sensuality of the wood's colors, patterns, and textures speak of timeless universal rhythms which repeat in all of nature,"[6] states William Hunter. The artist's container symbolically intersects with the vessel tradition but only in a figurative sense. Here the lush, beautifully finished wood provides a sensual and compelling complement to the curvilinear structure which resembles a DNA helix. Hunter's skillful piercing of the vessel's walls creates an optical relationship between the front and back, inside and outside of the form. Speaking of the regenerative effect of the creative process, Hunter states, "These pieces as art objects represent a microcosm of the universe and their purpose in my life is fundamentally meditative. Being able to devote time, emotion, intellect, and physical energy to the successful completion of a single piece is like rebirth each time."[7] In linking the conceptual element of the work with the creative process, Hunter describes a holistic experience.

For his *Pepper and Salt Mills* [4], William Leete offers a simple explanation: "Although physical aspects are a large concern with utilitarian

5
**Ed Moulthrop**
The Chalice of Agamemnon, 1996
H 10" x W 7" x D 7"
H 254 mm x W 177 mm x D 177 mm
Wild black cherry wood
lent by the artist

6
**Helen Shirk**
Sustaining Spirit XV, 1995
H 8" x W 24" x D 24"
H 203 mm x W 609 mm x D 609 mm
Copper, patina, prismacolor
lent by the artist

Spiritual Context     37

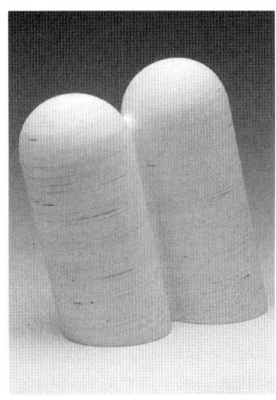

7
**Richard Hooper**
White Bipod, 1995
H 14" x W 14" x D 5"
H 355 mm x W 355 mm x D 127 mm
Birch ply
lent by the artist

8
**Hugh McKay**
Pentapot #2, 1996
H 16 1/2" x W 18" x D 15"
H 419 mm x W 457 mm x D 381 mm
Madrone burl
lent by Dr. Irving Lipton

design, I feel this work primarily evokes an emotional and spiritual response of graceful movement."[8] Leete's beautifully abstracted forms complement one another. Their subtle call-and-response relationship infers a feeling of harmony that is in keeping with spiritual principles.

The visual character of wood can connote a great many things. Nowhere is this more apparent than in the rugged but refined execution of Ed Moulthrop's *The Chalice of Agamemnon* [5], which offers a powerful, visceral metaphor for the life of the Mycenean general in whose honor the drinking vessel is named. For Moulthrop, "Wood is the most 'exquisite' of all materials. It has warmth, color, personality, and a history of its life revealed in its rings and stains."[9] As the artist uses it here, the deeply sculpted exterior and precisely finished interior underscore the physical and intellectual realm of the soldier.

Helen Shirk's richly variegated forms, lovingly colored with earthen tones inspired by the Australian bush, are notable for their ellipsoidal and spiraling vortex configurations. For the artist, the serial forms *Sustaining Spirit VIII and XV* [6] "... Symbolized a number of things, all intangible and powerful — nature, instinct, beauty, sanctuary, the primal, the non-rational and the mysterious."[10] The anomalous ordered forms are striking for their undulating contours and subtle beautifully marked surfaces.

### Abstraction

Abstraction can offer a powerful metaphor to engage spiritual ideas. Richard Hooper, for example, creates forms whose appearance are the epitome of simplicity, order, and transcendence. *White Bipod* [7] and *Vector Warp* are charged with irony, and they are compelling for their apparent remoteness from nature. Yet, each form's visual and tactical allure is due in large part to the natural materials from which it is made and whose intrinsic qualities are heightened by the artist's fine craftsmanship. The artist's inclination to exploit abstraction stems, as he says, from the genre's ability to "... Hint at archetypes or universals."[11] Such thinking

9
**Mike Shuler**
Gabon Ebony Bowl #818, 1996
H 5" x Diam 12 1/8"
H 127 mm x Diam 306 mm
Gabon ebony, choc-te-kok, cocobolo, Brazilian tulipwood, goncalo alves
lent by the artist

10
**Gord Peteran**
Untitled So Far, 1996
L 20" x W 7" x D 7"
L 508 mm x W 177 mm x D 177 mm
Leather, wood, linen thread
lent anonymously

is, here, clearly expressed. While initially we might take delight from the execution of such pieces, inevitably, we are left to confront the notion of origins, whether derived from theory or spirit.

Hugh McKay's *Pentapot #2* [8] also plays upon the notion of abstraction as a vehicle for ethereal ideas. Whether inspired by the structure of life viewed at a subatomic level or by the apparently simple but aberrant order of living things, McKay's use of repetition betrays an existence in which an inherent, endless continuity or holism endures. According to McKay, "I am seeking a certain power of expression through extreme stylization and expressionistic deformation in my work. The forms that I choose to find artistic expression with can be viewed as a material demonstration of an aversion to reality. This material demonstration is also a physical manifestation of a belief in an elsewhere."[12]

In *Gabon Ebony Bowl* [9] the notion of contained energy, light, and spirit, can be inferred from the sensitive combination of woods, whose complementary qualities offer a contrast to those of the ebony wood vessel. Mike Shuler describes his intentions: "These works exist for their own purposes of carrying imagery of beauty, infinity and order that hopefully will inspire the mind and feed the human spirit."[13] Perhaps an homage to the Gabon of Africa, *Gabon Ebony Bowl* is dramatic for its combination of dark and light woods, metaphors for the worlds of the unknown and the familiar.

Notions of the extraordinary and everyday, the symbolic and the conspicuous are evocative dualities which artist Gord Peteran explores in *Untitled So Far* [10]. In an overt sense, Peteran's work is perhaps the furthest removed from the tradition of turning. But it is precisely the wood turning practice to which the artist is dedicated and to which he labors to ascribe deeper significance. He obscures, but does not take away from us, our ability to discern the turned work's shape. Instead, Peteran encases the form in an alternative, seductive material. In so doing, he jars our senses, provokes us to question the piece's merits in this context and causes us to search deeper still for commonalties. Ultimately, the artist's motive is

11
**Robin Wood**
Nest of Pole-Lathe Turned Bowls, 1995
H 5" x Diam 13"
H 125 mm x Diam 325 mm
Spalted Beech
lent by the artist

one of faith, belief in the process. According to the artist, "My piece is a response to the process of surfacing that occurs as a turned object is excavated from within the log. This resulting dichotomy sets up a quizzical tension between what is seen, what is felt, and what is hidden."[14]

### Tradition and Ritual

Fulfillment, spiritually and otherwise, can be achieved in ways too numerous to catalog here. Yet, in the same way which we understand indigenous peoples to honor "Mother Earth" by taking from nature only that which will be used to sustain life, we can witness a similar intent in the pole-lathe turned bowls of Robin Wood. The product of a centuries-long tradition, pole-lathe turned bowls, such as the *Nest of Pole-Lathe Turned Bowls* [11] optimize the available material, thus affording an environmentally sensitive solution to the utilization of natural resources. Wood relies on the inherent visual effects lumber contains rather than those achieved through the inlaying of exotic woods or other such techniques. As the artist states, "It [this process] demands that the entire physical output of a strong person be concentrated on a tiny hidden cutting tool. The results are 'honest' bowls, designed to be functional whilst bringing a little beauty into everyday life."[15] In continuing a useful tradition and by uncovering nature's poetry, fixed year to year in the ebb and flow of the growing cycle, Wood taps into a sense of the eternal and the universal.

No less fraught with the challenges and pleasures of production are the arranged wooden table wares of Merryll Saylan. This artist's achievement is notable in that her output is overtly autobiographical. Saylan notes, "... These pieces are a celebration of being able to stand and turn, ... that hone my skills after a long period away from the lathe. They capture the essence of home and the simple things it contains."[16] Though the artist appears concerned with outward beauty and story telling, as evidenced by her use of the still life genre in *The Breakfast Tray* [12] and *Turning 60, 1:18, (work in progress)*, such arrangements, for the artist, pro-

12
**Merryll Saylan**
The Breakfast Tray, 1996
H 5" x W 23 1/2" x D 17"
H 127 mm x W 596 mm x D 431 mm
Maple
lent by the artist

voked inward meditation. According to Saylan, "The work is more narrative than I've done before and reflects the time spent in recovery from surgery, a time that afforded reflection ..."[17] The artist's sculptural compositions reflect an ordered existence, some might call obsessive. Nevertheless, such purity of intention can also be interpreted as a quest for fulfillment, expressed through the practice of ritual.

**Epilogue**

Perhaps the most compelling of findings here are the brilliant and vital manifestations of spiritual subjects expressed by turners in the turned object and through the turning process. In the period between humanity's first encounter with North America's forested landscape and today's suburban sprawl, our sense of nature is more often than not borne of secondhand experience. Today, our exposure to the outdoors is often just a momentary intervention in between environmentally secure work and domestic spaces and our automobiles or commuter facilities.

1  Thomas Cole, "Essay on American Scenery, 1835," in John W. McCoubrey, ed., *American Art 1700 – 1960 Sources and Documents* (Englewood Cliffs, NJ: Prentice-Hall, Inc., 1965): p. 8.
2  Ibid, p. 108.
3  Excerpted from Christian Burchard's statement to the jury.
4  Excerpted from Melvyn Firmager's statement to the jury.
5  Soetsu Yanagi, "Irregularity" in *The Unknown Craftsman: A Japanese Insight into Beauty* (New York: Kodansha America, Inc. and Kodansha International, 1972 and 1989): p. 122.
6  Excerpted from William Hunter's statement to the jury.
7  Ibid.
8  Excerpted from William Leete's statement to the jury.
9  Excerpted from Ed Moulthrop's statement to the jury.
10 Excerpted from Helen Shirk's statement to the jury.
11 Excerpted from Richard Hooper's statement to the jury.
12 Excerpted from Hugh McKay's statement to the jury.
13 Excerpted from Mike Shuler's statement to the jury.
14 Excerpted from Gord Peteran's statement to the jury.
15 Excerpted from Robin Wood's statement to the jury.
16 Excerpted from Merryll Saylan's statement to the jury.
17 Ibid.

## *Eye, Hand, and Mind*
## Turning as Art, as Craft, as History, as Thought

*David Revere McFadden*

David Revere McFadden was recently appointed Chief Curator and Vice President of Programs and Collections of the American Craft Museum, New York.

He was born on August 28, 1947 and received a BA in 1972 and a MA in 1978, both in Art History from the University of Minnesota. His studies were in Renaissance and Baroque studies and Chinese history.

McFadden was the Executive Director of the Millicent Rogers Museum of Northern New Mexico in Taos from 1995 to 1997 and the Curator of Decorative Arts and Assistant Director for Collections and Research at the Cooper-Hewitt Museum in New York from 1978 to 1995. He has curated over fifty exhibitions, including, *Wine: Celebration and Ceremony, Scandinavian Modern 1880-1980, Hair,* a visual and design history of human hair and *Structure and Style: Modernism in Dutch Applied Arts 1880-1930.*

McFadden has published over 70 books and articles worldwide. He has received numerous awards, including The Presidential Design Award for Excellence in 1994 and Chevalier de l'Ordre des Arts et des Lettres in 1989.

A facile and accomplished action of the hand, operating in seamless coordination with the eye, is frequently touted as a basic skill that defines excellence and talent in any craft. Historically, craft techniques, whether making use of wheels, looms, knives, or blowpipes, compose a global language that cuts across many boundaries of time and geography. Contemporary glassblowers can "read" the working methods of glassmakers from Syria in the first century B.C.E. Work from the studios of potters in Alfred, N.Y., today may comfortably and comprehensibly make reference to techniques, glazes, and forms developed in China centuries ago.

The *pas de deux* of eye and hand that establishes and nurtures a language of technique, however, should be melded with the active thought process, the intellectual content of making, into a choreographed trinity. Without understanding the role of thought in the creative process in both craft and art, the hand/eye relationship is diminished. As a result of turning's significance as a technique of industrial production in the nineteenth century, and its historical importance from the sixteenth century through the eighteenth century as an Enlightenment-inspired metaphor for social, political, and intellectual ideas and relationships, it holds a special place in defining the role of hand, eye, and mind in the creative process.

Like most traditional art historians, those who study craft, design, and decorative arts are prone to analysis, categorization, and classification as working techniques. With classification and analysis supported by conscientious study of both material and artistic cultural history, we may be able to illuminate the social basis of the art experience of makers as well as viewers. Relationships, themes, ideas, and concepts take on more importance than simple technical analysis, and result in a broader and more intriguing "relational database" of facts and ideas. These are the tools that help us move from the study of technique to the study of creativity.

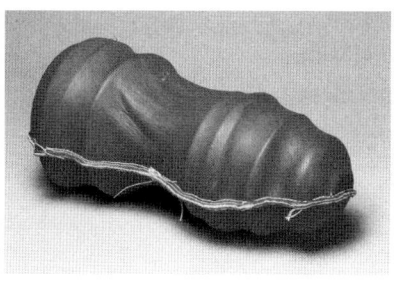

1
**Gord Peteran**
Untitled So Far, 1996
L 20" x W 7" x D 7"
L 508 mm x W 177 mm x D 177 mm
Leather, wood, linen thread
lent anonymously

Before writing this essay to accompany an exhibition of contemporary turning, hundreds of slides submitted by artists from around the world were viewed repeatedly over a three-day session with fellow jurors. These images became the raw material from which the curators selected the contents of this exhibition. Since that review period, weeks have passed; many objects have faded in my memory. while others are remembered clearly. Through *Untitled So Far*, Gord Peteran [1] has continued to allure, intrigue, and inform the content of this essay. This enigmatic object, at first glance, seems to be a large ornament, apparently turned, with a distinctive profile composed of interlocking convex and concave turns, much like a large chess pawn. The turned object is sealed, disguised, and yet revealed through a tightly stitched red leather case, a reliquary for a precious embalmed relic. The baroque contours of the object make the leather taut at stress points, and flaccid and yielding between the turnings. The texture, color, and suggestive shape tantalize the eye and hand, but the entombed object also reminds the viewer that the "real" object inside can never be touched, except with the imagination. Seeing, in this instance, is not about making, but about knowing. Knowing is much more than what is simply seen with the eye or even touched by the hand. This provocative object became a metaphor for the field of turning itself, and suggested that the technological, political and social history of the turner's art may still inform the aesthetics of turned objects today, underlining the interlocked worlds of hand, eye, and mind. The exhibition sought to balance the artistic and emotional aspects of turning with the exhilarating technical expertise revealed in the works, but also to recapture some of the rich intellectual history of the field.

All decorative arts — ceramics, glass, woodworking, metalworking, textiles — share a common history that interweaves technology and art. Technical expertise is necessary to transform humble clay into porcelain, silica sand into elegant blown glass, or rough unformed wood into masterpieces of the turner's art. Technical skills are developed over time and

2
**Hans Weissflog**
Rocking Bowls, 1995
each H 3 1/2" x W 6 3/4" x D 6"
each H 85 mm x W 170 mm x D 155 mm
Left one elm, right one pear
lent by the artist

through painstaking trial and error; decorative arts and design histories, particularly of centuries past, underline the importance of the education process and the value of cumulative practical knowledge. Technical knowledge usually implies a relationship with history. Developed by the artisan or craftsman, systematized in a series of logical relationships, and transmitted from one workshop or generation to another by means of direct teaching, oral and manual history, or by written documents, technical knowledge becomes a legacy, a heritage, and a scientific and cultural buttress.

The historical origins of turning can be traced back to the first millennium B.C.E., an event of significance to the history of technology preceded only by the invention of the potter's wheel and the bow drill. An Etruscan turned wooden bowl found in the Tomb of the Warrior at Carneto is pointed to as a foundation stone in the history of turning.[1] The earliest illustrations of turning lathes, however, do not occur until the sixteenth century, when turning was adopted and embraced as an appropriate occupation for sovereigns and aristocrats.[2]

From this point forward, the use of the lathe to create practical and useful objects such as bowls and balusters stands in stunning contrast to the use of this sophisticated machine to create objects of technical virtuosity and artistic merit.

The first major publication on the tools and techniques of turning was Charles Plumier's *L'Art de Tourner*, issued in 1701.[3] This volume includes seventy-nine detailed plates of machines and tools that provide the first comprehensive reference manual for both practical turners and those "amateurs" interested in the artistic possibilities of turning. Divergent paths of practical turning and artistic turning are already established in Plumier's treatise. Plumier provides accurate technical information for turners of any type, but specifically targets those who wish to make works of art using the lathe. The intellectual history of turning is recorded in the adoption of the lathe and of the technique of turning beautiful and essentially useless objects by the aristocracy in the seventeenth and eighteenth centuries.

As the Director of the Danish royal collections at Rosenborg Palace, which boasts one of Europe's finest and most important courtly collections of turned objects made by members of the royal family, states, "princely education was (and still is) a very careful and varied thing, with the given purpose to prepare the young princes and princesses for their future roles. Turning has the further advantage that when first the prince has been taught to hold the knives, to place the patterns, to keep the object spinning, it is a comparatively easy process to create an object that looks like art."[4]

Indirectly, but assuredly, linked to this historical tradition of virtuosity and technical accomplishment are numerous turners working today, some of whom are represented in the present exhibition. Technical achievement, however, is gained and expressed at several different and distinctive levels. Hans Weissflog of Germany, whose *Rocking Bowl* [2] is a masterpiece of traditional virtuosity, creates an ever-changing moiré pattern of line and space in miniature, suggesting the perpetual fascination with the ineffable and magical fantasies that the lathe both permitted and encouraged in the seventeenth and eighteenth centuries [3]. A more modern note using similar technique is struck by William Hunter in his *Dalbergia Cyclone* [4]. Hunter's technical mastery impresses most viewers immediately and directly. Does one look for deeper meaning as "art" from works such as these, or simply accept the performance of the work as its own artistic goal? In these works, technique is not a means to an end, but a viable end in itself, celebratory of process, of idea and hand working in concert, and of the glories of material transformation.

Another group of turners represented in the exhibition share a similar spirit of admiration for technique, taking the technical exuberance of Weissflog and Hunter but transforming it into something more contemplative and intellectual. Ernst Gamperl's thinly turned bowls, with

3
Inv.no 23-5: Ivory, 1764, Turned by L. Spengler, the figures of the corpus by G. Wolframm, and the topfigure by J.E. Bauert

3
Inv.no 6-393: Ivory, before 1718. The cipher CA = Christian Albrecht of Gottorp.

Intellectual Context    45

3
Inv.no 12-192: The lathe of Queen Sophie Magdalene, designed by D. de Thurah, 1735-36.

3
Detail
Inv.no 12-192: The lathe of Queen Sophie Magdalene, designed by D. de Thurah, 1735-36.

their moebius-like edges, capture and hold both air and light in a fragile shell of wood. Their simplicity and spareness is achieved only through reduction of physical mass and visual weight; these are objects of meditation at the same level as the teabowl in the tea ceremony. Another layer of thought is conveyed by Lincoln Seitzman's [5] extraordinary trompe l'oeil bowls and vases that mimic the intricate basketry of Native American artisans. Not only do Seitzman's works toy playfully with our sense of materials and techniques, they underline the frailness of knowledge achieved by sight alone. These are works that tell us that we must know, as well as see, to fully understand. Knowing, in this case, also includes a knowledge of the process and materials, revealing the sympathies and also the differences between baskets and turned objects.

For seventeenth and eighteenth century royal turners, whose extraordinarily complex and accomplished turnings adorn the walls of palaces from Denmark to Germany and Russia, and for whom specially designed and ornamented turning lathes were built for use in the royal chambers, modern distinctions between technique and art, which form the basis of both debate and controversy in the field of turning today, simply did not exist. Technical skill and knowledge, rather than being regarded as a means to another (more noble?) end of making art, were inseparable from art itself. In our century, it has been difficult, if not impossible, to extricate ourselves from the perennial and exhausting debate surrounding the differences between art and craft. Our love of this debate, which places art on one elevated end of the spectrum, and contrasts it with craft (handcraft, minor arts, decorative arts, call them what you like) at the opposite end, has distorted our ability to recognize that the intellectual content of making things — the physical, mechanical, logical, and manipulative processes that shape any material — is not necessarily separate from the process of art-making.

The making of objects with aesthetic, spiritual, and emotional merit, in the past as well as today, cannot be divorced from the technology

4
**William Hunter**
Dalbergia Cyclone, 1995
H 6" x W 11" x D 11"
H 152 mm x W 279 mm x D 279 mm
Cocobolo rosewood
lent by Ruth and David Waterbury

that serves as an underpinning for the art. Turning is, by its own definition, dependent upon the machine. According to one of the most recent and provocative writers on the intellectual, social, and political history of turning, the technique was "nothing other than the illustration of *ars naturam superat*," (art over nature).[5] As such, turning served as an effective metaphor for society itself, absorbing and encoding a mode of thought and action appropriate to guiding human and political affairs. Turning was, to a great extent, an earthly manifestation of a divine system and order, and as such became a metaphor for a world view. Turning was a way of training and educating future rulers, but also a way for rulers to express their power and virtue.

The historian Klaus Maurice writes,

"The machine was both metaphor and model for an age in which everything was subjected to a mechanistic way of thinking, in which everything was attributed to a mechanical function. Every physician and philosopher thought the world moved like a huge piece of clockwork ... The state was a large mechanical automaton ... the princes became springs, weights or balance wheels ... The prince at the lathe was not practising an everyday technique but was working at a piece of apparatus designed specifically for his role. A machine like the prince's lathe was rarely to be found in the craftsman's workshop. The prince learned how to shape a raw material to plan, how to perform regular controlled sequences, and without effort he identified himself with the idea of transferring mechanical causality to controlling the way society functions."[6]

If turning was once a useful metaphor for understanding and explaining a larger world of the spirit, does the same process of thought inform turning today? This, I believe, may be one of the fundamental issues raised by the present exhibition. What guiding principles inform and inspire the work of turners today? Is technical mastery a means to an end, or is it a critical factor in the asthetics of turned objects of our times? In past centuries, as I have suggested, rifts between art and technique may

Intellectual Context

5
**Lincoln Seitzman**
Storm Clouds Tray – Basket Illusion,
1995
H 2" x Diam 25"
H 50 mm x Diam 635 mm
Maple, paint, ink
lent by the artist

not have been so compelling or necessary as they are today. How do the turners themselves resolve the technical requirements of their chosen field with the aesthetic goals and pressures applied to them as they move from craft into art? A review of some selected exhibition pieces may be useful.

A small but noteworthy group of objects were submitted by turners working in a mode that can only be described as traditional handcraft. Robert Sonday's vessels carry rich tactile associations with traditional turning, revealed in richly textural surfaces that proclaim process as paramount. Robin Wood's *Nest of Pole-Lathe Turned Bowls* [6] goes one step further by not only suggesting tradition, but evoking it in a series of replicas of bowls from the Mary Rose shipwreck, all created on the traditional pole-lathe. Are such works more than continuations or repetitions of the familiar? With Wood's work in particular, it is the intellectual knowledge of the tradition, the knowledge of history, that the viewer brings to the work that gives it such life and power. Thought and vision, memory and imagination, are brought together in the work. These exquisitely turned "bowls of memory" serve as a wonderful counterpart to Merryll Saylan's hauntingly beautiful *Turning 60, 1:18 (work in progress)* [7] group of bowls, plates, and dishes. Saylan captures the abstract quality of memory, of time, and of history in these poetic and suggestive forms, proving humble traditions can be summoned to evoke strong emotions and powerful memories.

Klaus Maurice suggests that a part of the pleasure (and significance) of turning for courtly amateurs in the seventeenth and eighteenth centuries was the control over process, circumstance, and effect that turning nourished. He writes about the "fascination for the psychological phenomenon of a predetermined course, a course that was programmed and, therefore, ordered to the exclusion of anything else."[7] This fascination with the control and predetermination of effect offered by turning has not been overlooked by turners working today. For example, Mark Salwasser's *Wood Bullets* [8] are clearly derived from a twentieth-century

9
**Helen Shirk**
Sustaining Spirit XV, 1995
H 8" x W 24" x D 24"
H 203 mm x W 609 mm x D 609 mm
Copper, patina, prismacolor
lent by the artist

transformed by the technology to new plateaus. For the new generation of turners now emerging on the scene, however, the most important element is that so forcefully conveyed by the signature work for this essay.

The true potential of turning remains mysteriously hidden inside a skin of culture, history, and time. We perceive its outline, we are drawn to its forms, but its full significance and potential may yet be revealed and understood.

1. The literature of turning, including many technical manuals, was assembled by S. G. Abell and W. G. Ogden, Jr., as *A Bibliography of The Art of Turning and Lathe and Machine Tool History* (North Andover, Mass., The Museum of Ornamental Turning Ltd., 1987). A useful and basic introduction to the field that puts lathe technology and history into a broader context is L. T. C. Rolt, *Tools for the Job: A History of Machine Tools to 1950* (London: HMSO, 1965, rev. ed. 1986).

2. Many European collections of turned objects, made of ivory, wood, amber, and other semi-precious materials, remain unpublished. Among the most important collections of aristocratic turnings is that found in the Grünes Gewölbe (Green Vaults) of Dresden, assembled by Augustus the Strong, Elector of Saxony. The most recent publication dealing specifically with the turned works in this collection is D. Syndram et. al., *Wiedergewonnen: Elfenbein Kunststücke aus Dresden* (1995). Other collections, such as the major archive of turned works produced at the Danish court at Rosenborg Palace in Copenhagen, have not been fully published.

3. Plumier, Charles. *L'Art de Tourner ou de faire en perfections toutes sortes d'ouvrages au tour. Composé en Français et en Latin en faveur des Etrangers.* (Lyon: Chez Jean Certe, Marchand Libraire rue Mercière, 1701.) This landmark volume, the first to provide thorough documentation of the techniques and tools of turning, became extremely popular in the eighteenth century. As the bibliographers Abell and Ogden point out, the volume became the standard treatise for a century, (op cit, p.77). Plumier was translated into German, Russian, and Dutch, the Russian edition was specifically commissioned by Peter the Great. The volume cited in this essay is that translated by Paul L. Ferraglio as *The Art of Turning* (privately printed: 1975).

4. Letter dated 12 November 1996 from Dr. Mogens Bencard, director of De Danske Kongers Kronologiske Samling in Copenhagen, to author.

5. Maurice, Klaus. *Der drechselnde Souverän; Materialin au einer furstlichen Maschinkunst/ Sovereigns as Turners; Materials on a Machine Art by Princes.* Trans. D. A. Schade (Zürich: Verlag Ineichen, 1985): 7-8.

6. Ibid., 140-141.

7. Ibid., 7.

Intellectual Context 51

# How and Why

*William P. Daley*

William P. Daley is a ceramic artist and educator who lives in Elkins Park, Pennsylvania. He was born on March 7, 1925 in Hastings-on-Hudson, New York.

Daley received a BS from the Massachusetts College of Art, Boston, Massachusetts in 1950 and a MA from Columbia University-Columbia Teachers College, New York in 1951. His honors include election into College of Fellows, American Craft Council in 1988 and The College Art Association of America Distinguished Teaching of Art Award in 1991.

Exhibits include *Craft Today U.S.A.* in 1989 and a solo exhibition at Helen Drutt Gallery, New York in 1990. His work was published in *American Potters: The Work of Twenty Masters* by Garth Clark and *Ceramics: A Potters Handbook*, 5th edition by Glen C. Nelson

Daley's artwork can be seen in numerous public collections, among them, the Philadelphia Museum of Art, Pennsylvania, the Los Angeles County Museum of Art, California and the Victoria and Albert Museum in London, England.

The American philosopher Suzanne Langer in her books, *Philosophy in a New Key* and *Form and Feeling*, calls artists "formulators of symbols." As poets, musicians, painters, potters, and turners we "formulate symbols" that "do something for us" by creating our "life of feeling." She speaks of two kinds: discursive symbols that tell of facts and nondiscursive ones that speak of feelings. I like the distinction because it defines us as makers who develop thoughts and feelings by formulating symbols as material.

Sometimes, the things we make serve discursive ends, such as bowls or platters that work by holding food.[1] Other times, they work as symbols to evoke feelings as engaging orbital sculpture.[2] Most of the time, the things we make work simultaneously in both domains and are doubly useful.[3] When objects "do something for us" they operate on many levels and speak to our tactile, spatial, visual, and temporal intelligence as well as the more accessible and didactic, discursive aspects of knowing.

To better understand my own intentions, I sometimes separate doing into opposite pairs like study and work, studio or class, clay or drawing, making and thinking. I often see the opposites as active and passive or as "how" and "why." For me, "how" most often deals with fact and "why" with feelings. I see "how" connected to the studio and being about technology as skill, mastery, and outcome when I am making things. I think of "how" as the outside of doing and "why" as the inside. "Why" is the inner lining made up of nonverbal nondiscursive feelings. Feelings that are signaled by touch, temperature, tempo, and balance to direct knowing by the physicality of material. Mediating these feelings through material is what craftsmen-becoming-artists do. They make connections between technology's "how" and the artist's "why." For me, joining this inside-outside duality directs the tempo for the dance of our hands and mind with material.

Forgive my romantic subjectivity about making materials work for me. Playing formulation games with Langer's dual symbols by hooking them up to technology, "how" and "why" may be so numbing to you that they prove the case that turning the useful things people need is more than enough reason for a lifetime of honest work. The history of invention and its connections to necessity would support such a judgment. However, my observations jurying the *Challenge V: International Lathe-Turned Objects* exhibition would not. The majority of pieces there were about forming feelings rather than making discursive function their primary concern. There were many distinctive pieces that used technology to develop their feelings by using "how" to express "why."

Some work did this by combining old and new moves to make persuasive geometries. Others used new moves to speak deeply about the inherent qualities of turned material. Most of the work was about shaping feelings through material, even when the pieces had a functional intention. This body of great work describes for me a turners' renaissance that is grounded in the successes of individual craftsmen making their place by working as artists to discover their own voice.

Almost two decades ago, at a George School Wood Turning Symposium, I remarked on the connections between clay and wood to centrifugal form: it's all a matter of making bumps and holes to give form to spirit. Watching the progress since then, I marvel at the singular diversity of so many engaging voices that speak so convincingly of turners' exploration of bumps and holes.

Turners are the most recent of the ancient shapers of materials called craftsmen to begin the exhilarating, disquieting, and sometimes painful metamorphosis of becoming artists. They have changed our perceptions of their craft from a method of twentieth-century industrial production to an emerging art form. From the mechanical replication of historic models and the creation of nostalgia, turners have reinvented their traditions through the innovations of individuals. They have also looked to sculpture and other art forms as models to discover orbital geometries in nature. There isn't space here to enumerate the sources of inspiration and

1
**Max Krimmel**
Vessel #398, 1996
H 6 5/8" x Diam 13 1/5"
H 167 mm x Diam 335 mm
Colorado alabaster, satine
(bloodwood)
lent by the artist

1
**Merryll Saylan**
Turning 60, I:18
(work in progress), 1996
Maple
H 8" x W 26" x D 16"
H 203 mm x W 660 mm x D 406 mm
lent by the artist

2
**Hugh McKay**
Pentapot #2, 1996
H 16 ½" x W 18" x D 15"
H 419 mm x W 457 mm x D 381 mm
Madrone burl
lent by Dr. Irving Lipton

the turners who have worked them. Suffice it to say that their collective exchanges, transmutations, and recombinations have created an exciting moving center that is a promising platform for future venturing.

So this is a fitting time, at the Curators' Focus: *Turning In Context* exhibition, to think about the next century of turning as an art form. We are all at the same place. The potters, metalsmiths, and other object makers are all worrying. We have prospered by extending our hands and adapting this century's technology to amplify our touch. Now, ironically, as our successful building of mind-hand connections are being recognized, they are being challenged. Digital technologies are threatening and frightening us with the chimera of an electronic finger eating away our grandchildren's hands.

I don't know about the outcome. I have fears that are mixed with curiosity and stirred with desire to live to know what we make out of them. On my best days, I see this electric machine I'm writing on as a tool. On my dark days, I sink in its dreary possibilities. Despite my aging delusions, in my deepest gut I cannot help feeling that if one digit is the symbol for the fickle finger, five fingers make a hand. After all, counting on two of them is the original hand-mind connection of ten that started all this talk about "how" and "why."

My conversations with artist friends about our future seem to also have a good-day and bad-day quality about them. The talk is too elaborate to go into here, but let me sketch out a few scenarios. One of the most popular good-day themes is that we — the "maker material artists" or whatever we call ourselves then — will be the keepers of our culture's hands. We will be artist holdouts working to preserve the arts and crafts movement and hopefully prosper in the next century by keeping alive our traditions. At one extreme perhaps becoming Hand Luddites, turning away in communes to work and passively wait. Or, more plausibly, we will continue a scenario that is already well under way: a scenario that uses all the digital electronic capabilities — the software, and the hardware — to free

2
**Richard Hooper**
Vector Warp, 1995
H 12" x W 12" x D 5"
H 304 mm x W 304 mm x D 127 mm
Birch ply
lent by the artist

our days to be artists. We could become artists who work with our hands and offer the things we make to the world on the Internet. An old acquaintance of mine is already working hard to make his fortune by helping this happen. A bad-day phone caller told me a day ago that a highly respected gallery owner recently stated in a lecture that our craft movement, the one that privileges the hand, is over. The lecturer said the hand-mind connection will become the mind-tool connection and the satisfactions shared with our audience will merely be those of a designer.

I hope it doesn't work out that way. I am sure it will not. I think William Morris would be surprised and elated by touring all the venues from street fairs to SOFA to see the scale and variety of ways that hand workers have adapted to the preemptive technology of this closing century. I think we have used them well to create. It is my hope that we can get past dread, and become frightened enough to do more about the things we have started so we can show others how important we are to the future. We need to re-educate our communities about the connections between art and thought, between making things and cognition. We need to persuade our legislators about the need for formation as well as information to assure vibrant outcomes. The proofs are there about how learning takes place. Thanks to hooking up computer simulations to working brains in Parallel Distribution Processing studies. They show that the brain is modular and that Multiple Intelligence is not just a pedagogical buzz word.

Daniel Dennet, a cognitive scientist in *Consciousness Defined*, poses theories that hypothesize a contingent consciousness that brings brain cell populations within reach of an individual's felt mental states and responses. These theories prove that the brain is not hard-wired like a computer and reassert the nonlinear, nondiscursive aspects of cognition inherent in art production. We also know that the billions of neurons in the brain's

3
**Hans Weissflog**
Rocking Bowls, 1995
each H 3 1/2" x W 6 3/4" x D 6"
each H 85 mm x W 170 mm x D 155 mm
Left one elm, right one pear
lent by the artist

modules at birth disappear over time if they are not used. The connections between the hand and the cognitive functioning of the brain are not romanticized poetry.

A double irony is that we are being challenged by a technology that is helping to prove our case while art programs for our children are being cut in an "either-or" war between computer literacy and arts education. Earlier on, I said we were beginning to do some good things. Arrowmont has summer craft classes for kids. So does Anderson Ranch. Haystack has a workshop for Maine high school students and their art teachers. Last summer, Penland held a two-week session for classroom teachers to learn to use crafts to improve their students' learning. The Wood Turning Center is going to grade schools giving demonstrations with table-top portable lathes. I know of many college craft departments that are giving intensive hands-on weekend workshops for art teachers. We have started: we realize our efforts are symbolic tokens that we hope will gain momentum and persuade the people in our communities to pay for public art education. I have urged everyone to adopt an art teacher. If every craft artist in the country did it, we could make a difference. I am enjoying doing my "In-House Field Trips" by getting students excused from other classes for a day to work with clay, their art teacher, and me.

It would be great if the Wood Turning Center, the AAW, The American Craft Council, SNAG, and NCECA would start related programs to intervene and help art teachers help kids learn to solve problems by making things with real materials. The prescriptions are clear, the need is great, the time is short.

We have done well in our century-long metamorphosis from craftspeople to artists. We have grown and learned to use the "how" of technology to form the "why" of our spirits. We have tempered fear through craft and shared our genius with distinction in works that speak of ourselves with clarity and grace. In the process, we have confirmed the ways of making thoughts, feelings, and beliefs become realities. Sharing

3
**William Hunter**
Dalbergia Cyclone, 1995
H 6" x W 11" x D 11"
H 152 mm x W 279 mm x D 279 mm
Cocobolo rosewood
lent by Ruth and David Waterbury

this understanding in all the ways that we can is our challenge for the next century. If we succeed in making these exchanges with the vitality of our present creations, we will be among the gate keepers of the future. We will have learned to help everyone live well by evolving from craftsmen to artists to teachers.

1  *Vessel #398* by Max Krimmel and *Turning 60, 1:18 (work in progress)* by Merryll Saylan
2  *Pentapot #2* by Hugh McKay and *Vector Warp* by Richard Hooper
3  *Rocking Bowl* by Hans Weissflog and *Dalbergia Cyclone* by William Hunter

# Turning, Now and Then

*Albert LeCoff*

Albert LeCoff is the co-founder and Executive Director of the Wood Turning Center. He studied at Antioch University, Philadelphia, Pennsylvania and received a BA in Arts & Crafts in 1975. He also undertook a wood-turning apprenticeship with Manny Erez, Philadelphia, Pennsylvania for two years. Born on December 29, 1950, he resides in Philadelphia, Pennsylvania.

LeCoff has organized symposia and exhibitions to promote lathe turning for more than twenty years. Recent exhibitions have included, *Challenge V: International Lathe-Turned Objects,* in 1994 which toured the US for three years and *Revolving Techniques: Clay, Glass, Metal, Wood* in 1992 which opened at the James A. Michener Museum, Doylestown, Pennsylvania. Conferences have included the *1993 World Turning Conference: New Perspectives on an Ancient Craft* co-sponsored by the Hagley Museum, Wilmington, Delaware, and *allTURNatives: Creating, Critiquing, Collecting* held at the Berman Museum, Collegeville, Pennsylvania in 1996.

LeCoff has given dozens of lectures and participated in panel discussions related to lathe turning.

Lathe turning experienced a revival in the 1970s by largely self-taught craftsmen, who rediscovered the techniques of the lathe, and were, therefore, somewhat enamored of technique. They also placed strong emphasis on revealing wood's natural beauty.

However, since those early days of the revival, the development of turning as a field, rather than just a technique, has been dramatic. Greater numbers of artists and craftsmen have turned to the lathe as an art-making tool, exponentially increasing their technical and expressive virtuosity.

At the same time, the turning field has welcomed new practitioners with backgrounds as sculptors, painters, machinists, and metal smiths. This cross-pollination of the field with new ideas, materials and processes has brought a higher level of artistic growth and further evolution to a nearly forgotten craft technique.

We are seeing a new art form emerge and establish itself. As the turning field continues to welcome increased participation from artists based in other fields; as it encourages new approaches, ideas, techniques, and materials; as it forges new connections in the international turning community; as it develops a stronger presence and more recognition in the art world, we will see a mature art form, which we cannot yet imagine, flower in the future.

The Wood Turning Center has sought, through the structure of Curators' Focus: *Turning in Context* to embrace the diversity of lathe turning today. The varying points of view of each curator, sometimes overlapping, sometimes contradictory, underline the diversity and richness of the field.

Much of the work in *Curators' Focus* is by artists who have practiced turning for many years and have transcended technique. This work represents true aestheticism for its own sake and it presents a vision of the world to its viewers. Using technique to convey spirit, the artists have invited us into a new perception of our world.

Many of the objects in this exhibition exemplify a new way of working in the turning field. Rather than beginning with technique and making improvements artistically along this line of progression, we see many artists beginning with ideas and then fleshing them out physically and materially. These artists approach turning as a means to an end, while the lathe is just another tool in the shop.

In the last twenty years, I have personally witnessed the flowering of the lathe turning field. Many years ago, we started the Wood Turning Center to foster the growth of this burgeoning art form. The field now has thousands of committed supporters. It is unspeakably gratifying to see the increased recognition of the field by art lovers everywhere.

With a renewed faith in the future of lathe turning; I anticipate more organizations around the world promoting lathe turning, more exhibitions, more training and residency programs, more books and histories and publications, and a new facility for the Wood Turning Center's collections, workshops, and offices. Most of all, I like seeing artists of the international turning community increasing in numbers, working together, and growing artistically.

# Boris Bally

Weightlifting paraphernalia is not usually the source of craft inspiration as is the more traditionally explored vessel, chair, or flatware set. This pair of weight conical forms has a very specific function quite remote from the dignified world of fine art and galleries.

Our decade is full of get-in-shape fervor. Most of the members of my gymnasium think of sculpting and forming in terms of vanity, fashion, health, and strength. I enjoy creating sculpture for use in this unglamorous, sweaty environment.

The *Rep Forms* create a conceptual blur of cyclic confusion. Dumbbells are designed to sculpt the body which has in turn sculpted the dumbbells. The set toys with the concept of repetition(s) and (re)cycling.

The materials used for this piece are appropriate for an inner-city gym: they are the gritty remains of once-legible traffic signage and through lathe-finishing acquire a raw elegance.

- **RESIDES** Pennsylvania, U.S.A.
- **BORN** January 22, 1961
- **EDUCATION** 1984 Carnegie Mellon University, Pittsburgh, Pennsylvania - BFA
- **SELECTED EXHIBITIONS**
  1994-1996 Recycle, Reuse, Recreate curated by Dorothy Spencer, touring Africa
  1992 & 1995 11th Silbertriennale Goldschmiedehaus, Hanau, Germany
  1994-1997 Challenge V: International Lathe-Turned Objects, touring exhibition
- **SELECTED AWARDS**
  1993 Fellowship in Crafts, Pennsylvania Council on the Arts
- **SELECTED COLLECTIONS**
  American Crafts Museum, New York
  Renwick Gallery, Smithsonian Institution, Washington D.C.
  Victoria and Albert Museum, London, England
  Wood Turning Center, Philadelphia, Pennsylvania

Boris Bally
**Rep Forms,** 1996
each L 22" x W 9" x D 9"
each L 558 mm x W 228 mm x D 228 mm

*Reused traffic signs, aluminum*
*lent by the artist*

Curators' Focus: *Turning In Context*

# Gottfried Böckelmann

My works intend in general:

1. The objects should be for using, not "*L'art pour l'art*".

2. The aim is a well-balanced construction. In my view, only a well-designed work should be made.

3. The reanimation of historical precedents is an important cultural duty.

| | | |
|---|---|---|
| • | **RESIDES** | Hildesheim, Germany |
| • | **BORN** | January 20, 1930 |
| • | **EDUCATION** | 1954 School of Art and Craft, Bielefeld, Germany - State diploma as designer |
| | | 1955 Dorthmund - Master's examination as wood turner |
| • | **SELECTED EXHIBITIONS** | |
| | | Ongoing exhibitions, Organization of the German Handcraft in Australia, Belgium, France, Japan, New Zealand, the Netherlands, Norway, Portugal, Sweden, Switzerland, United Kingdom, United States and Russian Republics. |
| | | 1986 National Exhibition, Göttingen, Germany |
| • | **SELECTED AWARDS** | |
| | | 1961 Gold Medal in the State Private of Bavaria and special exhibition at the International Craft Exhibition in Munich, Germany |
| | | 1980 Order of Merit of Lower Saxony, Golden Service Cross of the Craftsman, Bonn, Germany |
| • | **COLLECTIONS** | |
| | | Museum of Art and Craft, Berlin, Germay |
| | | Museum of Art and Craft, Frankfurt, Germany |
| | | Wood Turning Center, Philadelphia, Pennsylvania |

Gottfried Böckelmann
**Bowl,** 1996
H 2 5/8" x W 4 3/8" x D 4 3/8"
H 72 mm x W 110 mm x D 110 mm

*Boxwood*
*lent by the artist*

Gottfried Böckelmann
**Box**, 1995
H 4" x W 3 3/8" x D 3 3/8"
H 100 mm x W 87 mm x D 87 mm

*Amboina*
*lent by the artist*

Gottfried Böckelmann
**Box f. Petschaft,** 1996
H 6" x W 5" x D 2 ¾"
H 152 mm x W 128 mm x D 72mm

*Black pine
lent by the artist*

# Christian Burchard

I enjoy the utter simplicity of the spherical shape, so full of significance for us. Below us; above us.

- **RESIDES** Oregon, U.S.A.
- **BORN** February 2, 1955
- **EDUCATION** 1974-1975 Furniture Apprenticeship, Hamburg, Germany
  1977-1978 School of the Museum of Fine Arts, Boston, Massachusetts
  1978-1979 Emily Carr College, Vancouver, British Columbia
- **SELECTED EXHIBITIONS**
  1997 Expressions in Wood: Masterworks from the Wornick Collection, Oakland Museum of Art, Oakland, California
  1995 Turned Wood '95, del Mano Gallery, Los Angeles, California
  1994-1995 Turning Plus..., Arizona State University Art Museum, Tempe, Arizona
  1994-1997 Challenge V: International Lathe-Turned Objects, touring exhibition
  1991 Turned Vessels Defined, Society of Arts and Crafts, Boston, Massachusetts
- **SELECTED COLLECTIONS**
  Los Angeles Folk and Craft Museum, Los Angeles, California
  Royal Cultural Center, Jedda, Saudi Arabia
  Wood Turning Center, Philadelphia, Pennsylvania

Christian Burchard
**Dance,** 1996
H 6" x W 6" x D 6 1/4"
H 152 mm x W 152 mm x D 158 mm

*Osage orange, paint*
*lent by the artist*

# Christopher Darway

The machine lathe was used in two stages of this work. I first turned a fabricated tube and dome to true it up before completing the fabrication of my model. A rubber mold was made from the model for a lost wax casting of each element, this being a production piece. The second stage was the coiling of the stainless steel wire to form the spring. I made a simple wire feed fixture to mount on the tool holder. The gear train was set to ten threads per inch, and the wire was wound onto a mandrel at a very slow feed to produce springs.

With a little experimenting, I found the right diameter mandrel and wire gauge to produce the proper tension for the springs.

The ring is part of an ongoing series of rings which self-adjust to the wearer. *Push Button Ring* is especially satisfying to me because it meets several of my personal objectives: clean design, ease of production, wearability, and humor.

- **RESIDES** New Jersey, U.S.A.
- **BORN** June 20, 1947
- **EDUCATION** 1970 Philadelphia College of Art - BFA - Craft Design
- **SELECTED EXHIBITIONS**
  1996 Structure and Geometry, Nancy Sachs Gallery, Saint Louis, Missouri
  1996 Revelations, SNAG, Shipley Museum, Gateshead, England
  1995 Five Chinese Elements, The Trenton City Museum, Trenton, New Jersey
  1994 Invitational Cup Show, Works Gallery, Philadelphia, Pennsylvania
- **SELECTED AWARDS**
  1994-1995 Artist Fellowship, New Jersey State Council on the Arts
  1994 Niche Award

Christopher Darway
**Push Button Ring,** 1994
H 3" x W 3" x D 3"
H 76 mm x W 76 mm x D 76 mm

*14k gold, stainless steel, wood
lent by the artist*

# Dennis Elliott

*Shallow Open Bowl* is a traditional bowl form with an undulating rim, stepping down to a smooth inner rim. This piece reveals the beautiful figuring of the burl with its smooth interior finish and unobstructed large opening. It was turned on the lathe and then carved.

- **RESIDES**      Connecticut, U.S.A.
- **BORN**      August 18, 1950
- **EDUCATION**      1972 Started turning wood. Self-taught.
- **SELECTED EXHIBITIONS**
  
  1997 Expressions in Wood: Masterworks from the Wornick Collection Oakland, Museum of Art, Oakland, California
  
  1995 The Banquet American Craft Museum, New York
  
  1994-1995 Turning Plus..., Arizona State University Art Museum, Tempe, Arizona
- **SELECTED COLLECTIONS**
  
  The Mobile Museum of Art, Mobile, Alabama
  
  Museum of Fine Arts, Boston, Massachusetts
  
  Renwick Gallery of the Smithsonian Institution, Washington, D.C

Dennis Elliott
**Shallow Open Bowl,** 1995
H 6 1/2" x Diam 21"
H 165 mm x Diam 533 mm

*Big leaf maple burl
lent by the artist*

## Jack T. Fifield

I feel this piece best fits the intellectual context. It is representative of the evolution of my involvement with wood turning. The block of myrtle wood was formed in the back of an old man's pick-up in 1951 (I was two years old). I suppose it spoke to me for I hadn't turned on a lathe since 1972 and didn't own a lathe, yet I knew I must turn this block. The myrtle wood waited in a Tennessee barn while I was engaged in the study of natural form. I didn't even realize I was studying to be a wood turner. I gained an appreciation, fascination really, for the small-mouthed hollow forms of potters and the open curvilinear symmetry of basketry.

With the help of my friend Rude, I became the owner of a "General" lathe. My hands knew what to do, and my mind let them. Anatomy: delicate lips, broad shoulders — sharply defined, gentle curve of the belly, hips, small feet; dynamic balance; careful hollowing, thin and smooth; time irrelevant, nonexistent.

- **RESIDES** Kentucky, U.S.A.
- **BORN** March 10, 1949
- **EDUCATION** 1995 Rude Osolnik Workshop, Poverty Ridge, Berea, Kentucky

  1971-1974 University of Minnesota School of Dentistry, Minneapolis, Minnesota

  1972-1975 Cedar Workshop, Minneapolis, Minnesota - apprenticeship
- **SELECTED EXHIBITIONS**

  1997 Henderson Fine Arts Center, Henderson, Kentucky

  1996 Kentucky Guild 35th Anniversary, Giles Gallery - EKU, Richmond, Kentucky

  1996 Kentucky Guild of Artists and Craftsmen Spring Show Berea, Kentucky

  1995 Making It Special, Louisville Visual Arts Association, Water Tower Gallery, Louisville, Kentucky

  1994 Shared Path: Works by Jack and Linda Fifield, Contemporary Artifacts Gallery, Berea, Kentucky

Jack T. Fifield
**Myrtle Burl: Hollow Form,** 1996
H 6 1/2" x Diam 12"
H 165 mm x Diam 304 mm

*Myrtle burl*
*lent by the artist*

Curators' Focus: *Turning In Context*

# Melvyn Firmager

My *Seaflower* series is produced from a material (eucalyptus gunnii) so unstable it is regarded as useless lumber. Working with this wood has been just about the most exciting thing I have done in wood turning. The wood changes shape when I work it, creating tensions not otherwise experienced in most turning activities. Producing such work with nature playing an equal and dramatic part has had a profound effect on me.

This piece is called *Seaflower* because the waves represent seaweed, fins, and sea itself. Waves and spirals are the same, just seen from a different perspective —

The very essence of life.

The empty vessel represents the womb and the female form —

The very essence of life.

It is symbolic of where we came from, our spirituality, the Goddess within.

On another level, it is fun. It makes people smile and laugh.

- **RESIDES**      Somerset, England
- **BORN**      March 25, 1944
- **SELECTED EXHIBITIONS**
  1996 del Mano Gallery, Los Angeles, California
  1993 Newburger Gallery, SUNY, Purchase, New York
  1992 Craft in Action, St. Donat's Castle, Llantwit Major, South Glamorgan, Wales
- **SELECTED COLLECTIONS**
  The Contemporary Museum in Honolulu, Hawaii
  Dr. Irving Lipton, Los Angeles, California
  Anita and Ron Womick, Burlingame, California

Melvyn Firmager
**Seaflower #340,** 1996
H 4 1/2" x Diam 5"
H 114 mm x Diam 127 mm

*Ebonized eucalyptus gunnii
lent by Dr. Irving Lipton*

# Ernst Gamperl

For the past seven years the vessel has been the focus of my creative work.

I do not recognize arbitrary limitations that are often accordingly cited.

For me, the quest for balance between form and materiality is again and again a new challenge.

| | | |
|---|---|---|
| • | **RESIDES** | Vesio di Tremonsine, Italy |
| • | **BORN** | February 4, 1965 |
| • | **EDUCATION** | 1986-1989 Apprentice cabinet-maker |
| | | 1991-1992 Wood turning course with Professor Gottfried Böckelmann, Hildesheim, Germany |
| | | 1992 Master in Wood Turning, Hildesheim, Germany |
| • | **SELECTED EXHIBITIONS** | |
| | | 1994 (Inter)National Wood Turning Exhibition Victoria, Australia |
| | | 1994 6th Triennial of Contemporary German Arts and Crafts, Museum of Applied Art, Frankfurt, Germany |
| | | 1995 Gallery Slavik, Vienna, Austria |
| • | **SELECTED AWARDS** | |
| | | 1994 Final Winner Best Piece of Show - (Inter)National Woodturning Exhibition & Competition, Victoria, Australia |
| • | **SELECTED COLLECTIONS** | |
| | | Danner Foundation, Munich, Germany |
| | | National Museum of Württemberg, Stuttgart, Germany |

Curators' Focus: *Turning In Context*

Ernst Gamperl
**Bowl,** 1996
H 5 ¾" x Diam 7 ⅛"
H 145 mm x Diam 180 mm

*African ebony*
*lent by the artist*

Ernst Gamperl
**Bowl**, 1996
H 7 1/8" x Diam 15 3/4"
H 180 mm x Diam 400 mm

*Sycamore, maple, walnut
lent by the artist*

## Bob Hawks

Most of my ideas for turned pieces come from things I have seen that had some motion involved. This piece was inspired by a fountain that had water flowing up from the center and cascading gently over the sides. I call it *Norfolk Challenge* because it is made from Norfolk Island pine and was very difficult to execute.

- **RESIDES** Oklahoma, U.S.A.
- **BORN** May 10, 1920
- **EDUCATION** Art Center College in Los Angeles, California
- **SELECTED EXHIBITIONS**
  1996-1999 Turn, Turning, Turned
  1996 VISIONMAKERS Oklahoma Arts Commission in Oklahoma City and Bartlesville, Oklahoma
  1996 Regional Craft Biennial, Arkansas Art Center, Little Rock, Arkansas
  1994-1997 Challenge V: International Lathe-Turned Objects, touring exhibition
- **SELECTED COLLECTIONS**
  Simmons Foods of Siloam Springs, Arkansas
  The White House, Washington D.C.
  Wichita Art Museum in Wichita, Kansas

Bob Hawks
**Norfolk Challenge,** 1995
H 5 1/2" x Diam 16 1/2"
H 139 mm x Diam 419 mm

*Norfolk Island pine*
*lent by the artist*

# Richard Hooper

*White Bipod* is an extrapolation of a double hemispherical form into two parallel cylindrical forms. This piece attempts to explore biomorphic archetypes in a futuristic idiom. I wanted to create a hybrid organic form in a mechanistic vein. It was influenced by my interest in science fiction imagery.

*Vector Warp is* an exploration into the visual "warping" effect of curved strata. It reflects my interest in the concepts of astrophysics, such as bending properties of light, time, mass and space, and the possibility of the existence of parallel worlds.

- **RESIDES** Childwall, England
- **BORN** March 29, 1958
- **EDUCATION**
  1995 Wood Turning Center - International Turning Exchange Residency
  1982 Buckinghamshire College of Higher Education, High Wycombe, Buckinghamshire, England, Furniture Design and Technology - MA
  1980 Exeter University, College of St. Mark and St. John, Plymouth, Devon, England, - Bachelor of Education in Design
- **SELECTED EXHIBITIONS**
  1994-1995 Turning Plus..., Arizona State University Art Museum, Tempe, Arizona
  1994 Works off the Lathe, Concord Gallery, University of Liverpool, England
  1994 Nimbus Gallery, Benedict Arts Centre, Liverpool, England
  1994-1997 Challenge V: International Lathe-Turned Objects, touring exhibition
- **SELECTED AWARDS**
  1996 Grant - Foundation for Sports and the Arts
- **SELECTED PUBLICATIONS**
  1996 American Woodturner, March edition
  Drechseln, Germany, Spring edition

Richard Hooper
**White Bipod,** 1995
H 14" x W 14" x D 5"
H 355 mm x W 355 mm x D 127 mm

*Birch ply*
*lent by the artist*

Richard Hooper
**Vector Warp,** view 1, 1995
H 12" x W 12" x D 5"
H 304 mm x W 304 mm x D 127 mm

*Birch ply*
*lent by the artist*

Richard Hooper
**Vector Warp,** view 2, 1995
H 12" x W 12" x D 5"
H 304 mm x W 304 mm x D 127 mm

*Birch ply*
*lent by the artist*

# Stephen Hughes

The third in the *Vader Box* series — this piece shows a technical mastery of turning on two separate axis. It is a lidded form that represents man's need to find a balance between technology and the delicate nature of the globe we live on.

| | | |
|---|---|---|
| • | **RESIDES** | Aspendale Gardens, Australia |
| • | **BORN** | December 20, 1958 |
| • | **EDUCATION** | 1980 Melbourne State College, Melbourne, Australia, B.Ed in Secondary Arts and Crafts |
| • | **SELECTED EXHIBITIONS** | |
| | | 1997 Expressions in Wood: Masterworks from the Wornick Collection Oakland Museum of Art, Oakland, California |
| • | **SELECTED AWARDS** | |
| | | 1995 First Prize - National Woodturning Exhibition and Competition, Australia |
| • | **SELECTED COLLECTIONS** | |
| | | Dr. Irving Lipton, Los Angeles, California |
| | | Wood Turning Center, Philadelphia, Pennsylvania |

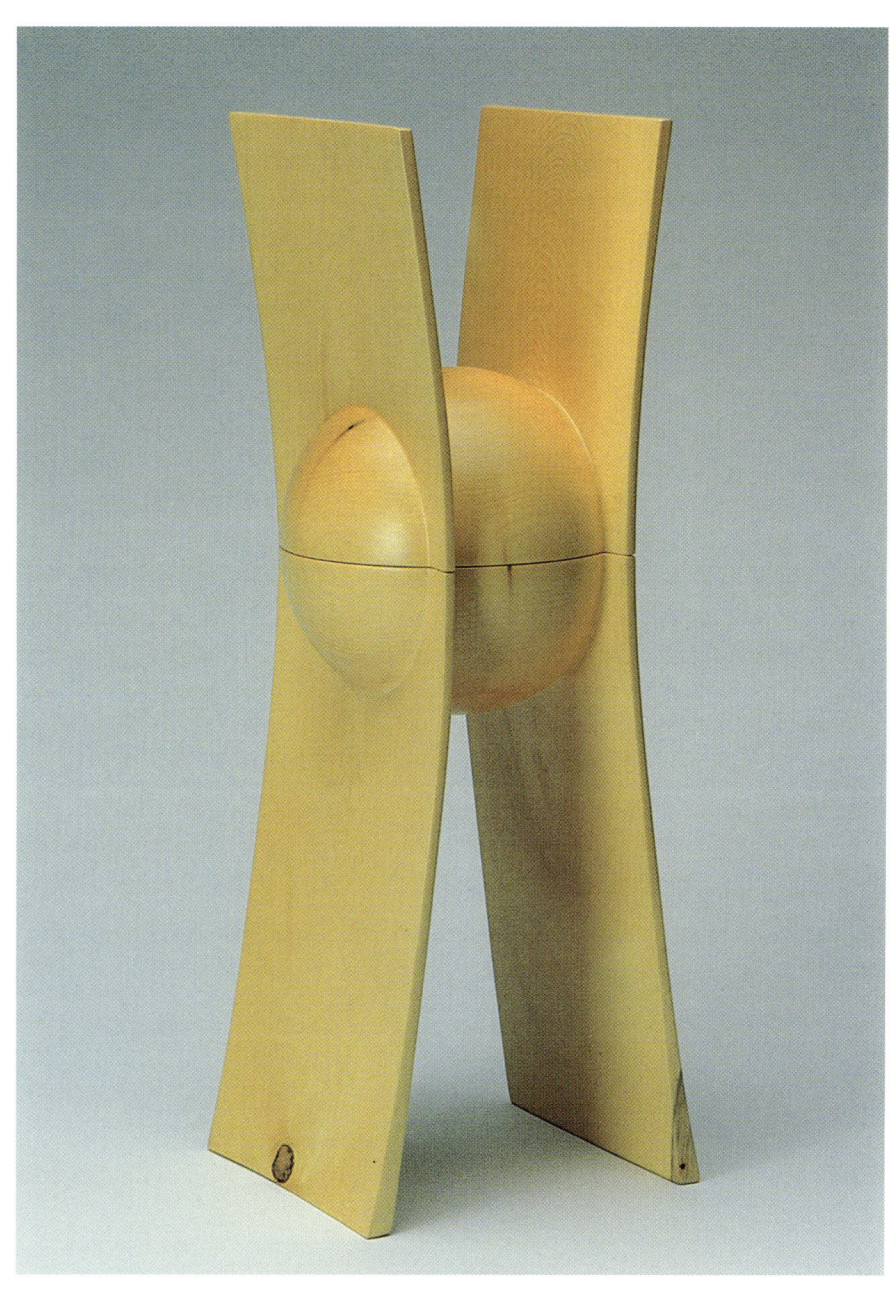

Stephen Hughes
**Vader Box III,** 1995
H 15 ¼" x W 5 ½" x D 5"
H 387 mm x W 140 mm x D 127 mm

*Huon pine*
*lent by the Wood Turning Center*

Curators' Focus: *Turning In Context*

# William Hunter

The motive for *Dalbergia Cyclone* is interplay, not only between interior and surface, front and back, top and bottom, positive and negative, but also light and shadow ... reality and illusions. How these intermingle as the piece is revolved or the viewer moves causes the patterns of these relationships to take on a continuously shifting, morphing life. The result is a conflict between what is perceived and what is thought to be true.

I have always been inquisitive regarding the nature of the various materials with which I've worked. What is inherent? What is suggested? What is possible? Through the manipulation of traditional turning methods and with the addition of previously unrelated carving techniques I can get to the visual language where I speak best. If an object I've made is true, it should be a vehicle of engagement, recognized viscerally, independent of language.

- **RESIDES** California, U.S.A.
- **BORN** October 15, 1947
- **EDUCATION** 1968 Santa Monica City College - AA - Fire Science
  1971 California State College/Dominguez Hills
  BA - Sociology/20th Century Thought
- **SELECTED EXHIBITIONS**
  1997 Expressions in Wood: Masterworks from the Wornick Collection, Oakland Museum of Art, Oakland, California
  1996 Nature Turning into Art, The Carleton Art Gallery, Carleton College, Northfield, Minnesota
  1995 Three Generations of Woodturners: The Making of an Art Form, Connell Gallery, Atlanta, Georgia
  1994 -1997 Challenge V: International Lathe-Turned Objects, touring exhibition
  William Hunter-Turned Wood, Okun Gallery, Santa Fe, New Mexico
- **SELECTED COLLECTIONS**
  American Craft Museum, New York
  High Museum of Art, Atlanta, Georgia
  Oakland Museum, Oakland, California
  Wood Turning Center, Philadelphia, Pennsylvania

William Hunter
**Dalbergia Cyclone,** 1995
H 6" x W 11" x D 11"
H 152 mm x W 279 mm x D 279 mm

*Cocobolo rosewood*
*lent by Ruth and David Waterbury*

# Ron Kent

Nature has contributed rich spalting and exciting knot patterns to this log. I have sought a design that interacted with natural patterns to best advantage. The "floating" silhouette imparts a seeming lightness that emphasizes the bowl's translucent walls.

- **RESIDES**     Hawaii, U.S.A.
- **BORN**     May 18, 1931
- **EDUCATION**     1957 University of California Los Angeles - BSME
- **SELECTED EXHIBITIONS**
  1997 Expressions in Wood: Masterworks from the Wornick Collection, Oakland Museum of Art, Oakland, California
  1992 Out of the Woods (FAMOS), touring exhibition, Europe
  1987 Craft Today, USA, Europe and USA
- **SELECTED COLLECTIONS**
  American Craft Museum, New York
  Detroit Institute of Art, Detroit, Michigan
  The Louvre, Paris, France
  Metropolitan Museum of Art, New York
  The White House, Washington D.C.

Ron Kent
**Floating Bowl,** 1996
H 8" x Diam 16"
H 203 mm x Diam 406 mm

*Norfolk Island pine*
*lent by the artist*

# Peter Kovacsy

Warm and sensual, this work evokes an emotional response from its viewer. Captive in its nature and by design the vessel symbolizes emotional being, that place within each of us that is moved by personal will.

The emotional make up of each viewer will create a unique response for everyone. While some feel harmony and beauty in the work, others will project quite negative values upon it. Emotions are human expressions and are colored by each individual's reactions to experience in life. The enigma is that we are the ones with emotions and the artwork is just a catalyst, an object quietly existing without any awareness of our presence or emotions.

- **RESIDES** Pemberton, Australia
- **BORN** May 7, 1953
- **EDUCATION** 1968 Special Arts Program, Applecross Senior High School, Perth, West Australia
- **SELECTED EXHIBITIONS**
  1996 Small Treasures, del Mano Gallery, Los Angeles, California
  1994-1995 Turning Plus..., Arizona State University Art Museum, Tempe, Arizona
  1994-1997 Challenge V: International Lathe-Turned Objects, touring exhibition
  1993 Conservation by Design, Rhode Island School of Design, Providence, Rhode Island
  1993 Australian Contemporary Furniture Exhibition, Beaver Galleries, Canberra
- **SELECTED COLLECTIONS**
  Dr. Irving Lipton, Los Angeles, California
  Alice Springs Craft Acquisition, Craft Council of the Northern Territory, Australia

Peter Kovacsy
**Emotions Series — Wood You Like Me To Seduce You,** 1993
H 3" x Diam 12 1/2"
H 76 mm x Diam 317 mm
*Sheoak, medium density fiber board, brass foil, lacquer*
*lent by the artist*

## Max Krimmel

What it's about is communication. I make objects because it's fun and, equally important, so that people experiencing the object get some idea of who I am or who I was. Depending on who they are, they may see a kindred spirit or a wild unfathomable presence.

Whether the same or different, they glimpse a person, with the usual set of encumbrances and facilities, working in 1996 and trying his best. With that in mind I attempt to communicate as close to the core of my reality as possible. What is left in the object, after elimination of artifice and decoration, is what I cannot get rid of and therefore the most basic to what I am.

- **RESIDES**    Colorado, U.S.A.
- **BORN**    October 2, 1948
- **EDUCATION**    1984 University of Colorado at Boulder - Fine Art
  1969 Colorado State University, Fort Collins, Colorado - Industrial Arts
  1966-1968 University of Denver - Design
- **SELECTED EXHIBITIONS**
  1995 Soup to Nuts, Wharton Esherick Museum, Paoli, Pennsylvania
  1995 The Art of Craft, Longmont Museum, Longmont, Colorado
  1994-1995 Turning Plus..., Arizona State University Art Museum, Tempe, Arizona
  1993 Form and Object: Contemporary Interpretations of Craft Traditions, Arvada Center for the Arts, Arvada, Colorado
- **SELECTED COLLECTIONS**
  Arrowmont School, Gatlinburg, Tennessee
  Wood Turning Center, Philadelphia, Pennsylvania

Max Krimmel
**Vessel #398,** 1996
H 6 5/8" x Diam 13 1/5"
H 167 mm x Diam 335 mm

*Colorado alabaster, satine (bloodwood)*
*lent by the artist*

# Stoney Lamar

The development and use of multiple axis techniques as a way of applying texture or sculpting asymmetrical forms on the lathe has allowed me to transcend the round object and to create a sense of image and movement. A multiple axis approach has also allowed me to draw from a wider range of influences and to develop a more personal imagery and narrative.

The work begins as a relationship with a particular piece of wood and how its characteristics interplay with my intentions and my emerging technical and conceptual vocabulary.

The resulting figurative, architectural, or abstract object is an attempt to create balance and tension by juxtaposing asymmetrical and symmetrical elements.

*Trinity* is part of a continuum of work preceded by the *Addicted to the Rhythm Series* and the *Vector Series*. These series are the most material and process influenced. They are simply variations on the rhythms and movement in wood as a craft material and wood turning as a craft process.

*Muse* represents influences both past and present. Most recently, the symmetry of the individual elements in some African masks has led me to an investigation of how a single line can express an emotion. *Muse* also represents a return to one of my earliest sculptural explorations — how concave surfaces can define a space beyond the object itself while convex surfaces tend to draw the object into itself.

- **RESIDES** North Carolina, U.S.A.
- **BORN** November 26, 1951
- **EDUCATION** 1979 Appalachian State University, Boone, North Carolina - BS
  1984-1985 Assistant to Mark and Melvin Linquist, New Hampshire Studio
- **SELECTED EXHIBITIONS**
  1995 Three Generations of Wood Turners, Connell Gallery, Atlanta, Georgia
  1994-1997 Challenge V: International Lathe-Turned Objects, touring exhibition
  1994 Fall Colors, Blue Spiral 1, Asheville, North Carolina
  1992 Fifth Annual Lathe-Turned Objects Show: Stoney Lamar, Sansar Gallery, Washington D.C.
- **SELECTED COLLECTIONS**
  Arkansas Museum of Art, Little Rock, Arkansas
  High Museum of Art, Atlanta, Georgia
  Renwick Museum, Smithsonian Institution, Washington D.C.
  Wood Turning Center, Philadelphia, Pennsylvania

Stoney Lamar
**Trinity,** 1996
H 13" x W 14" x D 6"
H 330 mm x W 335 mm x D 152 mm

*Madrone*
*courtesy of Connell Gallery*

Stoney Lamar
**Muse,** 1996
H 15" x W 13" x D 12"
H 381 mm x W 330 mm x D 304 mm

*Madrone*
*lent by Robyn and John Horn*

# William Leete

This pair of salt and pepper mills is the fifth in a series of designs where I have adapted my large-scale sculpture to utilitarian tableware. My intent is that these forms read as elegant spirits of seasoning with brightness relating to their respective contents. Utilitarian constraints include a means to turn the mill, which is afforded by the arm element; a means to adjust the mill, which is accomplished by turning the head; and a containing area for pepper or salt; and the mill mechanism in the body. The bottom is funnel-shaped to ease filling with pepper or salt. For strength and ease of production, the threads in the head and the square hole in the arm were cast in epoxy.

Although physical aspects are a large concern with utilitarian design, I feel this work primarily evokes an emotional and spiritual response of graceful movement. The diagonal body position and asymmetrical arms of these culinary spirits create a dance for one's dining pleasure.

- **RESIDES** Michigan, U.S.A.
- **BORN** March 30, 1950
- **EDUCATION** 1974 University of Wisconsin - MFA
  1972 University of Wisconsin - BS Art
- **SELECTED EXHIBITIONS**
  1994-1995 Turning Plus..., Arizona State University Art Museum, Tempe, Arizona
  1992 Lathe-Turned Objects Defined III: Functional and Sculptural, Society of Arts and Crafts, Boston, Massachusetts
  1991-1992 Challenge IV: International Lathe-Turned Objects, touring exhibition
  1990 Woodturning: Vision and Concept II, Arrowmont School of Arts and Crafts, Gatlinburg, Tennessee
- **SELECTED COLLECTIONS**
  Marquette General Hospital, Marquette, Michigan
  Arthur and Jane Mason, Washington D.C.
  National Design Museum, Smithsonian Institution, New York

William Leete
**Pepper & Salt Mills,** 1996
each H 10 1/2" x W 4 1/2" x D 2 1/2"
each H 266 mm x W 114 mm x D 63 mm

*Walnut, maple, steel, dye, bleach, wax, paint, sealer, epoxy lent by the artist*

Curators' Focus: *Turning In Context*

# John Macnab

I have been producing wood turnings since 1985.

My wood turnings of late are based on the intrigue and respect which I hold for machining.

I have a strong interest in historical and industrial machining techniques. I see it as an appropriate challenge to use equipment that dates from a previous time in the history of industry because of its still useful applications.

Likewise, I am equally enthusiastic about practices that are specific to contemporary machines. I am continually challenged to see what kinds of complex forms I can make by way of a new machine's capabilities.

Using an array of modern machines and techniques, sometimes numerically controlled, *Untitled* is more mathematical than most of my work. I think of it as more of a manifold than a vessel. It has become a model for a much larger piece presently under construction.

| | | |
|---|---|---|
| • | **RESIDES** | Nova Scotia, Canada |
| • | **BORN** | May 7, 1961 |
| • | **EDUCATION** | 1981 Nova Scotia Land Survey Institute - Cartography diploma |
| • | **SELECTED EXHIBITIONS** | |
| | | 1995 Once a Tree, Halifax, Nova Scotia, Canada |
| | | 1993 Zwicker's Gallery, Halifax, Nova Scotia, Canada |
| | | 1992 Northern Arizona University, Art Museum and Galleries, Flagstaff, Arizona |
| | | 1992 Craft and Folk Art Museum, Los Angeles, California |
| | | 1991 North West Gallery of Fine Woodworking, Seattle, Washington |
| | | 1991 University Art Museum, Arizona State University, Phoenix, Arizona |

John Macnab
**Untitled,** 1996
H 17 1/2" x W 5" x D 5"
H 444 mm x W 127 mm x D 127 mm

*Black walnut (spent veneer core), ebony
lent by the artist*

# Laura Marth

I am most concerned with conveying an emotion or a personality with my work. The majority of my work is narrative and deals with the tension created between a controlled, manipulated medium and an expressed emotion which seems to have no business being there. I am attracted to the irony of this and drawn to works which address this. I am also a lover of craft and its sibling, machining. I am drawn to the incredible beauty of a well-made machine in action. I am caught in a spiral: a love affair with emotion, craft, and machines. It is an endless spiral that has no conclusions, only new frontiers.

- **RESIDES**  Wisconsin, U.S.A.
- **BORN**  June 17, 1956
- **EDUCATION**  1987 Kent State University, Kent, Ohio - MFA
  1980 Massachusetts College of Art, Boston - BFA
- **SELECTED EXHIBITIONS**
  1995 The Joanne Rapp Gallery, Scottsdale, Arizona
  1995 To See or Not to See, Nancy Sachs Gallery, St. Louis, Missouri
  1995 From the Lathe, Brookfield Craft Center, Brookfield, Connecticut
  1994-1997 Challenge V: International Lathe-Turned Objects, touring exhibition
  1994 The Teapot, Museum of American Crafts, New York
- **SELECTED AWARDS**
  1995 Art Fellowship, Pennsylvania Council of the Arts
- **SELECTED PUBLICATIONS**
  1994 Metalsmith, fall volume 14, Number 4

Laura Marth
**The Red Velvet Love Seat,** 1994
H 10" x W 2 ½" x D 2 ½"
H 254 mm x W 63 mm x D 63 mm

*Anodized aluminum pepper mill and salt shaker (2 elements) lent by Fleur Bresler*

## Hugh McKay

I am seeking a certain power of expression through extreme stylization and expressionistic deformation with my work. The forms that I choose for artistic expression can be viewed as a material demonstration of an aversion to reality.

This material demonstration is also a physical manifestation of a belief in an "elsewhere." The work connects with human imagination and acting as a lens or a window to this place.

My work is also a demonstration of a belief that something of a mundane and servile status (the crafted vessel intended for use in this case) can rise above all accepted explanations for its purpose. Hence the apparent uselessness of my wood pots. They do not have an acceptable reason for being in this reality. They belong "elsewhere."

| | | |
|---|---|---|
| • | **RESIDES** | Oregon, U.S.A. |
| • | **BORN** | December 27, 1951 |
| • | **EDUCATION** | 1970-1973 Southern Oregon State College |
| | | Self-taught woodworker |
| • | **SELECTED EXHIBITIONS** | |
| | | 1996 A Madcap Teapot Party at the Renwick, Renwick Gallery, Smithsonian Institution, Washington D.C. |
| | | 1995 Turned Wood Craft and Folk Art Museum, Los Angeles, California |
| | | 1994 Delaware Center for Contemporary Arts, Wilmington, Delaware |
| | | Turned Wood '94, del Mano Gallery, Los Angeles, California |
| | | 1994-1997 Challenge V: International Lathe-Turned Objects, touring exhibition |
| • | **SELECTED AWARDS** | |
| | | 1996 International Turning Exchange Residency, Wood Turning Center, Philadelphia, Pennsylvania |
| • | **SELECTED COLLECTIONS** | |
| | | Ruth Greenburg, Los Angeles, California |
| | | Dr. Irving Lipton, Los Angeles, California |
| | | Wood Turning Center, Philadelphia, Pennsylvania |

Hugh McKay
**Pentapot #2,** 1996
H 16 1/2" x W 18" x D 15"
H 419 mm x W 457 mm x D 381 mm

*Madrone burl*
*lent by Dr. Irving Lipton*

# Stephen Mines

*The Silver Scepter* is a natural progression of the magic wands I've been turning for the last several years and explores the possibilities of ornamented spindle turning. The medium of aluminum for the scepter is new for me, as are the incorporation of a turned "case" in wood to hold/protect it, and a balancing base to display it.

*Physical Context:* Whether or not *The Silver Scepter* is viewed as an art or utilitarian object might be determined by the station in life of the person(s) possessing it. A sovereign might rightly use it as an emblem of authority, a magician as a prop, a "collector" as a pretty thing. That it is more or less a "traditional" object created by more or less "traditional" methods is obvious.

I should think any emotion evoked by viewing *The Silver Scepter* will certainly be particular to the viewer. I was emotionally involved in making it but not in an attempt to wring deep emotion from an observer. Meaning (meaningfulness) is in the eye of the beholder.

Bearing in mind that a scepter/magic wand is by its very nature meant to convey a sense of power, natural or supernatural, and has been employed throughout history to that end, *The Silver Scepter* can be seen in a spiritual context.

The form (wands, staffs, scepter, etc.) simply gives me something to define, redefine, and decorate, much as Fabergé used the egg form. I couldn't imagine making a Fabergé omelet, nor will I attempt to rule the San Fernando Valley with *The Silver Scepter*.

| | |
|---|---|
| • RESIDES | California, U.S.A. |
| • BORN | February 3, 1939 |
| • EDUCATION | 1957-59 Pasedena Playhouse College of Theatre Arts, Pasadena, California Certificate in Theatre Arts |
| | 1960 Choinard Art Institute, Los Angeles, California |
| • SELECTED EXHIBITIONS | |
| | 1994-1997 Challenge V: International Lathe-Turned Objects, touring exhibition |
| • SELECTED COLLECTIONS | |
| | Bruce Kaiser Collection, Wilmington, Delaware |
| | Dr. Irving Lipton, Los Angeles, California |
| • SELECTED PUBLICATIONS | |
| | American Woodturner, March 1994 |

Stephen Mines
**The Silver Scepter,** 1996
H 11" x W 37" x D 3"
H 279 mm x W 939 mm x D 76 mm

*Aluminum, cocobolo, synthetic rubies,
faceted crystal
lent by the artist*

## Connie Mississippi

"*Time Line — Ten Objects*" is a work in progress. Each of these pieces represents one year of the twentieth century. The entire work is comprised of 100 small sculptures, none larger than 12 inches. Each piece is accompanied by a notation of important events that occurred during the represented year.

Choosing to make a sculpture for each year of this century was a deliberate act of homage and discipline. Those years are what formed us as individuals and as a culture.

The materialization of an idea into an art object entails the searching, the thinking, and the making to find out what part of ourselves we as artists wish to communicate. Out of the billions upon billions of events which could have been chosen, the one I chose represents something particular to me and to my approach to this life and this time. These are what give the art its essence and what I send to the viewer.

- **RESIDES** California, U.S.A.
- **BORN** December 29, 1941
- **EDUCATION** 1972 Pratt Institute, Brooklyn, New York - MFA
  1963 Memphis College of Arts, Memphis, Tennessee - BFA
- **SELECTED EXHIBITIONS**
  1996 On and Off the Wall, Riverside Art Museum, Riverside, California
  1995 Turning in Space and Time, FIG Gallery, Santa Monica, California
  1995 Strictly Sculpture, Orange County Center for Contemporary Art, Santa Ana, California
  1994-1997 Challenge V: International Lathe-Turned Objects, touring exhibition
- **SELECTED COLLECTIONS**
  Fleur and Charles Bresler, Washington D.C.
  Rockefeller University, New York
  The White House, Washington D.C.

*Connie Mississippi*

Connie Mississippi
**Time Line — Ten Objects,** 1996
each H 8" x W 4" x D 4"
each H 203 mm x W 101 mm x D 101 mm

*Basswood, turned, carved, and painted
lent by the artist*

# Ed Moulthrop

Wood is the most exquisite of all materials. It has warmth, color, personality, and a history of its life revealed in its rings and stains.

It is the beauty and design of the wood itself which I try to utilize and reveal. Thus I work only with solid blocks of wood. Unlike clay, glass, metals and fiber, where the material is shifted and rearranged to the artist's desires, my works "have always been there." The wood you see is the wood exactly as it was created. I simply uncover it and there it is!

*The Chalice of Agamemnon* is a combined expression of the ancient vessel form, the archaic appearance of design and craftsmanship, and the look and feel of rich cherry wood. Both rough and highly finished in texture, the turning process is still apparent in the basic shape of the vessel and the precision and fine finish of the interior.

| | |
|---|---|
| **RESIDES** | Georgia, U.S.A. |
| **BORN** | May 22, 1916 |
| **EDUCATION** | 1938 Case Western Reserve University - B. Arch. |
| | 1941 Princeton University, Princeton, New Jersey - MFA |
| **SELECTED EXHIBITIONS** | |
| | 1992-1995 Arts America, U.S. Information Agency overseas exhibition |
| | 1994-1997 Challenge V: International Lathe-Turned Objects, touring exhibition |
| | 1987 High Museum of Art, Atlanta, Georgia |
| | 1986 Craft Today, Poetry of the Physical, American Craft Museum, New York |
| **SELECTED AWARDS** | |
| | 1987 Fellow, American Craft Council |
| **SELECTED COLLECTIONS** | |
| | Arkansas Art Center Decorative Arts Museum |
| | Metropolitan Museum of Art, New York |
| | Museum of Modern Art, New York |
| | Renwick Gallery, Smithsonian Institution, Washington D.C. |
| **SELECTED BIBLIOGRAPHY** | |
| | Who's Who in America |

Ed Moulthrop
**The Chalice of Agamemnon,** 1996
H 10" x W 7" x D 7"
H 254 mm x W 177 mm x D 177 mm

*Wild black cherry wood*
*lent by the artist*

# Jim Partridge

The more I think about it, the more I think these objects need to speak for themselves without analysis from the maker. I want to make objects that speak — or better still, sing — directly to their audience without the aid of footnotes.

| | | |
|---|---|---|
| • | **RESIDES** | Shropshire, England |
| • | **BORN** | June 29, 1953 |
| • | **EDUCATION** | 1977-1979 John Makepeace School for Craftsmen in Wood, Dorset, England |
| | | 1983-1984 Alsag College of Higher Education - Fellow in Wood, Chester, England |
| • | **SELECTED EXHIBITIONS** | |
| | | 1993-1994 Jim Partridge - Woodworker, Ruthin Crafts Centre, touring exhibition |
| | | 1993 Jim Partridge, from Brooches to Bridges, Site Specific Gallery, Arundel |
| | | 1990 Jim Partridge New Woodwork, The Scottish Gallery, Edinburgh, Scotland |
| • | **SELECTED AWARDS** | |
| | | 1986-1987 Grizedale Forest Sculpture Project - First Craftsman in Residence |
| • | **SELECTED COLLECTIONS** | |
| | | Kyoto Museum of Modern Art, Japan |
| | | Museum of Fine Arts, Boston, Massachusetts |
| | | Wood Turning Center, Philadelphia, Pennsylvania |

Jim Partridge
**Hard Mouthed Spode Form,** 1996
H 8" x W 8" x D 4"
H 203 mm x W 203 mm x D 101 mm

*Scorched burr oak*
*lent by the artist*

# Gord Peteran

I am not a "turner."

As a guest artist at a turning conference in Saskatchewan, Canada, I observed a great number of vessels released from their hiding places with an elegance and grace I had not previously observed. Often these works of art emerged from their cocoon within a very short time so that I was able to observe this transition in repetition.

My piece is a response to the process of surfacing that occurs as a turned object is excavated from within the log.

A block of wood was turned with large and random v-cuts. It was then bound in moistened leather and hand-stitched closed with linen thread. As the leather dried, it accentuated the high spots while leaving voids of stretched leather in the recesses partially revealing/obscuring the turning within.

The observer is blinded to the inner form by the very material that helps accentuate the gesture of its contents. The shape within cannot be trusted. Its undulating form between soft and hard, bound in the warm ox blood leader, is at the same time inviting and primal. This resulting dichotomy sets up a quizzical tension among what is seen, what is felt, and what is hidden. During the discovery process one is therefore compelled to familiarize oneself with the resulting form by handling it. Touch to see.

- **RESIDES**   Ontario, Canada
- **BORN**   September 22, 1956
- **EDUCATION**   1979 Ontario College of Art
- **SELECTED EXHIBITIONS**
  - 1995 Ontario Craft, Toronto, Ontario, Canada
  - 1994 Virtu National Juried Competition and Traveling Exhibition, Toronto, Ontario, Canada
  - 1993 From Start to Furnish, Contemporary Furniture Design Toronto, Ontario, Canada
  - 1992 A Treasury of Canadian Craft, Canadian Craft Museum, Vancouver, British Columbia, Canada
  - 1991 Art Furniture, Levinson Kane Gallery, Boston, Massachusetts
- **SELECTED PUBLICATIONS**
  - 1995 Globe and Mail, Design Section, November
  - Ontario Craft Magazine

Gord Peteran
**Untitled So Far,** 1996
L 20" x W 7" x D 7"
L 508 mm x W 177 mm x D 177 mm

*Leather, wood, linen thread*
*lent anonymously*

## Peter Pierobon

For some time I have been using the arcane language of Gregg shorthand to include hidden messages and commentary within the objects I make. On this lathe-turned object, I have incorporated a circular thought that (like the object housing it) never allows the eye or the mind to stop moving. The quotation reads, "Do you love me because I am beautiful, or am I beautiful because you love me?"

- **RESIDES**     Pennsylvania, U.S.A.
- **BORN**     April 9, 1936
- **EDUCATION**     1983 Wendell Castle School, Scottsville, New York - AOS - Furniture Design
  1976-1979 Capilano College, Vancouver, Canada - ceramics major
- **SELECTED EXHIBITIONS**
  1997 Expressions in Wood: Masterworks from the Wornick Collection, Oakland Museum of Art, Oakland, California
  1996 25 at 25, The Society for Contemporary Craft, Pittsburgh, Pennsylvania
  1995 Kathy Albers Gallery, Memphis, Tennessee
  1995 Please Be Seated: Masters of the Art of Seating, Flagler Museum, Palm Beach, Florida
  1994 Design for Living, Postwar Furniture from the Collection, Virginia Museum of Fine Arts, Richmond, Virginia
- **SELECTED AWARDS**
  1992, 1989 Individual Craft Fellowship Award, Pennsylvania Council on the Arts
  1988 Visual Artist Fellowship, National Endowment for the Arts

Peter Pierobon
**Do You Love Me Because I Am Beautiful, or Am I Beautiful Because You Love Me?**, 1996
H 36" x W 36" x D 4"
H 914 mm x W 914 mm x D 101 mm
*Ebonized mahogany*
*lent by the artist*

Curators' Focus: *Turning In Context*

# Mark Salwasser

I use woodcraft, primarily wood turning, to create propaganda. This body of my work is my editorial page.

Real bullets take 15 children from us every day. Put a *Wood Bullet* in your pocket, wear one on your lapel, hang one around your neck or from your ear to let people know where you stand on this issue.

- **RESIDES** Massachusetts, U.S.A.
- **BORN** August 7, 1947
- **EDUCATION** 1965-1971 California State University at Fresno - theater major
- **SELECTED EMPLOYMENT**
  1992-1993 Residency at the Old Schwamb Mill, Arlington, Massachusetts
- **SELECTED PUBLICATIONS**
  Design Book Seven, Fine Woodworking, Taunton Press, 1996
  AAW Journal 1997, Vol. 11, No. 4

Mark Salwasser
**Wood Bullets,** 1996
Life size

*Wood (50 elements)
lent by the artist*

## Merryll Saylan

Interest in Japanese presentation, ritual and form has influenced my work and most recently the drawings of Morandi, Diebenkorn and Thiebaud. The work has pushed me into learning more of the traditional techniques of wood turning and provided a way of honing skills after a long hiatus from lathe turning, though technical concerns without emotional content hold little interest for me. There has been great discomfort in moving my work in this direction yet a compelling need to create it.

My recent work, *The Breakfast Tray*, reflects the time spent in recovery from surgery, a time that afforded reflection, drawing and reading. The work is more narrative than I have done before and speaks of images and interconnections among home, family, and relationships. The work is directly connected to earlier work of sets of bowls and cases, trays with bowls, all sculptural units. Though that work was intended to be functional, in the still lifes I wish to present the power and beauty behind simple everyday things.

*Turning 60, 1:18 (work in progress)* incorporates several themes: my recent birthday and the number of years I am, getting back into the studio after a long hiatus, a celebration of being able to stand and turn, the essence of home and the simple things it contains. An element of spoof exists for me in the reference to videotapes and step-by-step instructions of turning projects devoid of emotional content.

- **RESIDES**  California, U.S.A.
- **BORN**  April 9, 1936
- **EDUCATION**  1979 California State University, Northridge, California - MA - Wood
  1973 University of California, Los Angeles, California - BA - Design
- **SELECTED EXHIBITIONS**
  1993 Contemporary Applied Arts, Summer Show, Convent Garden, London, England
  1993 Wooden Bowls, Galerie Fur Angewandte Kunst, Munich, Germany
  1992 The Hand and the Spirit, Women Woodturners, Joanne Rapp Gallery, Scottsdale, Arizona
- **SELECTED AWARDS**
  1990-1991 Artist in Residence, Grizedale, Cumbria, England, Northern Arts Council
- **SELECTED COLLECTIONS**
  Grizedale Forest Gallery, Cumbria, England
  Wood Turning Center, Philadelphia, Pennsylvania

Merryll Saylan
**The Breakfast Tray,** 1996
H 5" x W 23 1/2" x D 17"
H 127 mm x W 596 mm x D 431 mm

*Maple*
*lent by the artist*

Merryll Saylan
**Turning 60,
I:18 (work in progress),** 1996
H 8" x W 26" x D 16"
H 203 mm x W 660 mm x D 406 mm

*Maple*
*lent by the artist*

## Lincoln Seitzman

Physically, the design of *Storm Clouds* refers to the physical heavens — circular sky above, overlapping dark clouds, lightning zig-zagging between horizons. Proper execution of the design requires a thorough knowledge of the geometric properties of the circle. Depiction of a thunderstorm brings out feelings about raw nature: awe, fear and respect. If you stare intently at *Storm Clouds*, your focus will shift involuntarily from one cloud form to another. The clouds appear to be writhing. Is there a spiritual factor here? I leave it to you.

In *Yokut Snake Basket Illusion*, the olla-shaped vessel form is flattened to envelop snakes for rites. Yet the design snakes envelop the vessel. I sense some doubt here as to who controls whom, snakes or Indians. The vessel is apparently of coiled construction. Coiled baskets predate pottery. Coiled snakes predate both. Could snakes have provided the idea of the coiling process? Emotionally, snakes have always evoked strong feelings, — both fear and respect. Supernatural powers have historically been attributed to snakes.

- **RESIDES** New Jersey, U.S.A.
- **BORN** August 6, 1923
- **EDUCATION** 1943 Rensselaer Polytechnic Institute, Troy, New York - mechanical engineering
- **SELECTED EXHIBITIONS**
  1997 Expressions in Wood: Masterworks from the Wornick Collection, Oakland Museum of Art, Oakland, California
  1995 Turned Wood, del Mano Gallery, Los Angeles, California
  1995 Three Generations of Woodturning, Connell Gallery, Atlanta, Georgia
  1995 Illusions in Wood, Lathe Turnings by Lincoln Seitzman, Creations Gallery, Greenville, Delaware
  1994-1997 Challenge V: International Lathe-Turned Objects, touring exhibition
- **SELECTED COLLECTIONS**
  High Museum of Art, Atlanta, Georgia
  The White House, Washington D.C.
  Wood Turning Center, Philadelphia, Pennsylvania

Lincoln Seitzman
**Storm Clouds Tray —
Basket Illusion,** 1995
H 2" x Diam 25"
H 50 mm x Diam 635 mm

*Maple, paint, ink
lent by the artist*

Lincoln Seitzman
**Yokut Snake Basket Illusion,** 1993
H 10" x Diam 12"
H 254 mm x Diam 304 mm

*Oak, paint, ink*
*lent by the artist*

# Mark Sfirri
# Michael Hosaluk

We have worked together on various pieces since 1992. It has been very interesting to see how our collaborative path has traveled. We were invited to participate in an exhibition of teapots (of all things) at the Renwick Gallery in Washington D.C.

This was our second collaborative teapot. Michael made the pot and legs. When I studied it, I responded to the spherical shape. It reminded me of a balloon that was stretched to its limits and wanted to let out the air. I pictured a trumpet shape instead of a narrow pout for a teapot. From there the illusion grew with a mouthpiece and two valves. The painted imagery is meant to give emotion to the "figure." The typically unrelated objects of trumpet and teapot are brought together to create a new object that evokes humor and whimsy.

**MARK SFIRRI**
- **RESIDES** — Pennsylvania, U.S.A.
- **BORN** — August 1, 1952
- **EDUCATION** — 1978 Rhode Island School of Design - MFA
  1974 Rhode Island School of Design - BFA
- **SELECTED EXHIBITIONS**
  1993 The Mark and Mikey Show, Sansar Gallery, Washington D.C.
  1992 Lathe-Turned Objects Defined III, Society of Arts and Crafts, Boston, Massachusetts
  1991 Philadelphia Woodworkers, Pennsylvania Academy of Fine Arts, Philadelphia, Pennsylvania

**MICHAEL HOSALUK**
- **RESIDES** — Saskatchewan, Canada
- **BORN** — June 29, 1954
- **EDUCATION** — 1974-1975 Kelsey Institute of Applied Arts and Sciences Cabinet making and millwork, Saskatoon, Canada
- **SELECTED EXHIBITIONS**
  1991-1992 Challenge IV: International Lathe-Turned Objects, touring exhibition
  1994-1995 Turning Plus..., Arizona State University Art Museum, Tempe, Arizona
  1994 Whimsy, Canadian Craft Museum, Vancouver, British Columbia

Mark Sfirri / Michael Hosaluk
**Trumpot**, 1996
H 7 ½" x W 7" x D 5"
H 190 mm x W 177 mm x D 127 mm

*Maple and paint
lent by the artists*

Curators' Focus: *Turning In Context*

# Helen Shirk

When the possibility of six months in Western Australia became apparent, I welcomed the opportunity to leave my old life behind for a while and to experience a relatively isolated part of this huge continent. Australia gave me breathing space. It felt good to stand and stretch, take a deep breath, draw in the sights and sounds of a strange place. I am aware now that the Australian bush symbolized a number of things to me, all intangible and powerful — nature, instinct, beauty, sanctuary, the primal, the non-rational, and the mysterious. These two bowls encompass this world, forms push forward from the walls, vital and vivid, as if they were carrying life energy, the sustaining spirit. They serve as affirmations of survival, growth and connection.

- **RESIDES** California, U.S.A.
- **BORN** January 25, 1942
- **EDUCATION** 1969 Indiana University, Bloomington, Indiana - MFA
  1963-1964 Kunsthaandvaerkerskolen, Copenhagen, Denmark
  1963 Skidmore College, Saratoga Springs, New York - BS
- **SELECTED EXHIBITIONS**
  1996 Sculptural Concerns, Contemporary American Metalworking, California College of Arts and Crafts, Oakland, California
  1995 Helen Shirk: Contemporary Jewelry 1970 - 1995, Helen Drutt Gallery, Philadelphia, Pennsylvania
- **SELECTED AWARDS**
  1988 Visual Artists Fellowship, National Endowment for the Arts
  1963 Fulbright Grant to Denmark
- **SELECTED COLLECTIONS**
  American Craft Museum, New York
  Renwick Gallery, Smithsonian Institution, Washington D.C.
  Victoria and Albert Museum, London, England

Helen Shirk
**Sustaining Spirit VIII**, 1994
H 7" x W 20" x D 20"
H 177 mm x W 508 mm x D 508 mm

*Copper, patina, prismacolor
lent by the artist*

Helen Shirk
**Sustaining Spirit XV,** 1995
H 8" x W 24" x D 24"
H 203 mm x W 609 mm x D 609 mm

*Copper, patina, prismacolor*
*lent by the artist*

## Mike Shuler

*Gabon Ebony Bowl* is part of what I call Phase II of my work, a body of work that began nearly 12 years ago. The aspect of this that delineates it as Phase II is that patterning built into the object as polychrome, rather than the figure of the wood, establishs aesthetic values.

This is only one object in a long series, perhaps numbering in the thousands, that are stepping stones ultimately to large sculptural objects that will carry increasingly complex messages.

*Gabon Ebony Bowl* and other current works exist for the purposes of carrying imagery of beauty, infinity, and order that hopefully will inspire the mind and feed the spirit. The vessel form is useful for the time being, possibly because of the strong association between vessels and bodily nourishment.

- **RESIDES**  California, U.S.A.
- **BORN**  March 2, 1950
- **EDUCATION**  Life experience
- **SELECTED EXHIBITIONS**
  1996 Craft at Gump's: The Helen Heninger Years, San Francisco Craft and Folk Art Museum, San Francisco, California
  1995 Soup to Nuts, Wharton Esherick Museum, Paoli, Pennsylvania
  1994-1997 Challenge V: International Lathe-Turned Objects, touring exhibition
  1993 Holzschalen, Galerie fur Angewandte Kunst, Bayerischer Kunstgewerbe Verein Munich, Germany
  1989-1992 Craft Today USA, American Craft Museum and U.S. Information Agency European tour
- **SELECTED COLLECTIONS**
  American Craft Museum, New York
  High Museum of Art, Atlanta, Georgia
  Museum of Fine Arts, Boston, Massachusetts
  The White House, Washington D.C.
  Wood Turning Center, Philadelphia, Pennsylvania

Mike Shuler
**Gabon Ebony Bowl #818,** 1996
H 5" x Diam 12 1/8"
H 127 mm x Diam 306 mm

*Gabon ebony, choc-te-kok, cocobolo,
Brazilian tulipwood, goncalo alves
lent by the artist*

# Robert Sonday

In my work, I believe that making an exquisite but simple shape, then giving it texture ranging from glass-smooth beads to rough vertical cuts creates emotion.

Completing beaded surfaces which are as close to flawless as humanly possible, then taxing the surface with hand-incised texture, is a technically wonderful act. At any time the incorrect use of my skills and knowledge could give me nothing but a useless object.

If all phases come together, then an object which delights the visual and tactile senses is realized. That's what drives me in my work.

- **RESIDES** Virginia, U.S.A.
- **BORN** November 30, 1953
- **EDUCATION** Self-taught
- **SELECTED EXHIBITIONS**

    1994-1995 Turning Plus..., Arizona State University Art Museum, Tempe, Arizona

    1994-1997 Challenge V: International Lathe-Turned Objects, touring exhibition

    1993 Woodturning as an Art Form, Goldhaber-Fend Fine Arts Center Gallery, Johnstown, Pennsylvania

    1992 Treasures, John Michael Kohler Arts Center, Sheboygan, Wisconsin

    1989 Exhibition 280: Works Off Wall, Huntington Museum of Art, Huntington, West Virginia

- **SELECTED COLLECTIONS**

    Fleur and Charles Bresler, Washington D.C.

    Arthur and Jane Mason, Washington D.C.

    Tennessee State Museum, Nashville, Tennessee, for Edward Foss and Clinton Sisson

Robert Sonday
**Myrtle #4,** 1994
H 9" x Diam 7"
H 228 mm x Diam 177 mm

*Western myrtle*
*lent by the artist*

Robert Sonday
**Spalted Maple #14,** 1994
H 6" x Diam 7"
H 152 mm x Diam 177 mm

*Red maple*
*lent by the artist*

# Alan Stirt

We were originally asked to submit objects which related to the following contexts: the physical, the emotional, the spiritual and the intellectual. While these terms have clear meanings in the abstract, it is extremely difficult to apply them to actual objects. Like the word "art," these terms become hopelessly subjective when confronted with the real world. Within my own context, a piece must satisfy some emotional and spiritual need to be successful. It cannot do this without solid intellectual and physical credentials.

The carved pattern of the *Pine Needle Bowl w/Cut Rim* is a variation of a chevron pattern which is world-wide in distribution and goes back in time to the Old Stone Age. This pattern is used to create a rather chaotic rhythm in contrast to the stark symmetry of the turned form, relieved somewhat by the cut edge. The tension thus set up gives the piece a dynamic balance.

It is difficult for me to try to squeeze my work into anyone else's context. I have often found that a work that some others find deeply moving or spiritual can leave me cold. At best I can say that I make work that touches me emotionally or intellectually. I hope that it touches some others in a similar fashion. I work with bowl forms that are thousands of years old and seem to express an idea of beauty that cuts across cultural and temporal boundaries. I hope to have some aspect of myself come through in these pieces.

- **RESIDES** Vermont, U.S.A.
- **BORN** May 30, 1946
- **EDUCATION** Self-taught
- **SELECTED EXHIBITIONS**
  1995 The White House, Washington D.C.
  1994-1997 Challenge V: International Lathe-Turned Objects, touring exhibition
  1993 Tales and Traditions: Storytelling in Twentieth Century American Craft, Craft Alliance Gallery, St. Louis, Missouri
  1992 Out of the Woods: Turned Wood by American Craftsmen, Europe
- **SELECTED COLLECTIONS**
  American Craft Museum, New York
  Fine Arts Museum of the South, Mobile, Alabama
  High Museum of Art, Atlanta, Georgia
  The White House, Washington D.C.
  Wood Turning Center, Philadelphia, Pennsylvania

Alan Stirt
**Pine Needle Bowl w/Cut Rim,** 1996
D 3" x Diam 16 1/2"
D 76 mm x Diam 419 mm

*Maple, milk paint*
*lent by the artist*

# Randy Stromsoe

Soul mates if alive, these pieces are visually enhanced by the spatial relationship they share. On an emotional level they evoke images and feelings of trust, beauty, companionship — lovers, parent and child, dear friends.

- **RESIDES** — California, U.S.A.
- **BORN** — January 18, 1951
- **EDUCATION** — 1970-1973 Apprentice - Master Silversmith Porter Blanchard, Los Angeles, California

  1973-1975 Added training under Lewis A. Wise
- **SELECTED EXHIBITIONS**

  1995 Hot Tea, del Mano Gallery, Los Angeles, California

  1995 The White House Collection of Arts and Crafts, Smithsonian Institution, Washington D.C.

  1994-1995 Turning Plus..., Arizona State University Art Museum, Tempe, Arizona

  1994 Jewels and Gems/Collecting California Art, The Oakland Museum, Oakland, California

  1994-1997 Challenge V: International Lathe-Turned Objects, touring exhibition

  1993 Teapot Show, American Craft Museum, New York
- **SELECTED COLLECTIONS**

  The White House, Washington D.C.

Randy Stromsoe
**Pot à Crème et Cafetière,** 1996

H 13 ½" x W 6" x D 4 ½"
H 342 mm x W 152 mm x D 114 mm

H 16 ½" x W 8" x D 4 ½"
H 419 mm x W 203 mm x D 114 mm

*Pewter (2 elements)*
*lent by the artist*

# Hans Weissflog

After I turned my first ball box, I was looking for another interesting possibility to make a good-looking and complex ball box. *Ball Box with Rings* was turned around many different centers.

One day I wanted to make bowls — unusual bowls. I developed and turned *Rocking Bowls*. They consist of a combination of a very fragile part and a massive part, but made from one piece of wood, only on the lathe.

- **RESIDES** Hildesheim, Germany
- **BORN** January 20, 1954
- **EDUCATION** 1974-1976 Technikerschule Hildescheim, Germany, Machining
  1978-1982 Fachhochschule Hildesheim, Wood working and Design; Studied wood turning with Professor Gottfried Böckelmann
- **SELECTED EXHIBITIONS**
  1996 Turned Wood 96, del Mano Gallery, Los Angeles, California
  1995 Nature Turning Into Art, The Ruth and David Waterbury Collection of Turned Wood Bowls, The Carleton Art Gallery, Carleton College, Northfield, Minnesota
  1995 Avain Gallery, Helsinki, Finland
  1994 Closed Shapes - Wooden Object, Munich, Germany
  1994-1997 Challenge V: International Lathe-Turned Objects, touring exhibition
- **SELECTED COLLECTIONS**
  Corning Museum, Corning, New York
  Kunstgewerbe Museum (Museum for Arts and Crafts), Berlin, Germany
  Museum for Arts and Crafts, Cologne, Germany

Hans Weissflog
**Ball Box with Rings,** 1994
each Diam 2"
each Diam 50 mm

*Outside, African blackwood;*
*Inside, boxwood, (3 identical boxes)*
*lent by the artist*

Hans Weissflog
**Rocking Bowls,** 1995
each H 3 1/2" x W 6 3/4" x D 6"
each H 85 mm x W 170 mm x D 155 mm

*Left bowl elm, right bowl pear*
*lent by the artist*

# Robert S. Williams

The artist takes a turn ... a candlestick holder with a twist.

| | | |
|---|---|---|
| • | **RESIDES** | Pennsylvania, U.S.A. |
| • | **BORN** | February 14, 1956 |
| • | **EDUCATION** | 1974 Lincoln High School, Kimberton, Pennsylvania |
| | | 19 years experience in machine shop practices |
| • | **SELECTED EMPLOYMENT** | |
| | | present Turbo Research, Incorporated, Lionville, Pennsylvania, manufacturing products used in the power generating industry |

Robert S. Williams
**Untitled,** 1996
H 7 5/8" x Diam 3 1/4"
H 193 mm x Diam 82 mm

*Brass*
*lent by the artist*

# Robin Wood

*Nest of Pole-Lathe Turned Bowls* was made using the same technique that was used through all the centuries when wooden bowls were standard tableware. This technique demands that the entire physical output of a strong person be concentrated on a tiny hidden cutting tool. The results are "honest" bowls, designed to be functional whilst bringing a little beauty into everyday life.

*Pole-Lathe Turned Mary Rose Replica Bowl*, is a replica of a bowl found aboard Henry VIII's flagship the *Mary Rose*. Both the design and the production method of the bowl are the result of ten centuries of refinement during which time everyone in England ate from wooden bowls. The result is simple and beautiful but, above all, functional.

- **RESIDES** Sheffield, England
- **BORN** May 11, 1966
- **EDUCATION** 1983-1984 Kings College, London - studied biology
  1992-1993 Capel Manor Environmental Centre - City and Guilds Phase III, managing the countryside
- **SELECTED EMPLOYMENT**
  1996 Mary Rose Trust commission to produce replicas of their 450-year-old bowls and other turned items
  1995-present Self-employed as pole-lathe bowl turner
  1989-1996 National Trust Warden

Robin Wood
**Nest of Pole-Lathe Turned Bowls,** 1995
H 5" x Diam 13"
H 125 mm x Diam 325 mm

*Spalted Beech*
*lent by the artist*

Robin Wood
**Pole-Lathe Turned Mary Rose Replica Bowl,** 1996
H 2" x Diam 11"
H 50 mm x Diam 275 mm

*Beech*
*lent by the artist*

Curators' Focus: *Turning In Context*

**Wood Turning Center**

**Board of Trustees & Staff**

President
Bruce A. Kaiser

First Vice President
Fleur Bresler

Second Vice President
John Sherman

Treasurer
Lucy Scardino

Ron F. Fleming

Charles F. Hummel

Alan LeCoff

Connie Mississippi

Lincoln Seitzman

David Stephens

Executive Director
Albert LeCoff

Administrator
Susan Hagen

**Exhibition Committee**

Lisa Barnes

Edward Cooke

Stephen Hogbin

Charles F. Hummel

John Jordan

Stoney Lamar

Albert LeCoff

Lincoln Seitzman

**Credits**

**Editorial Staff**

Albert LeCoff, Editor

Judson Randall

Susan Hagen

Tina C. LeCoff

York Production Services

**Photography**

John Carlano
(all photos except the following)

Eric Mitchell, pages 12, 13, 14

Image, Wood Turning Center, page 15

Mark Sfirri, page 16

De Danske Kongers
Kronologiske Samling, pages 45, 46

David L. Smith, page 61

Tim Barnwell, pages 98, 99

Tom Brummett, page 119

**Design & Production**

Group M

**Printer**

PrintTech,
a division of York Graphic Services, Inc.